SUMMER BRIDGE LEARNING FOR
MINECRAFTERS

Bridging Grades 3-4

by Nancy Rogers Bosse
Illustrated by Amanda Brack

Sky Pony Press
New York

Visit our website at www.skyponypress.com.

Authors, books, and more at SkyPonyPressBlog.com.

10 9 8 7 6 5 4 3 2 1

Cover art by Bill Greenhead
Interior design by Kevin Baier
Interior art by Amanda Brack

All other art used by permission from Shutterstock.com

Print ISBN: 978-1-5107-4116-4

Printed in China

A NOTE TO PARENTS

You probably know the importance of having your child practice the key skills taught in the classroom. And you are probably hoping that your kid will be on board with practicing at home. Well, congratulations! You've come to the right place! *Summer Bridge Learning for Minecrafters, Bridging Grades 3–4* transforms learning into an adventure complete with zombies, skeletons, and creepers.

You will love that *Summer Bridge Learning for Minecrafters, Bridging Grades 3–4* aligns with the National Core Standards for math and English language arts (ELA), as well as national, state, and district recommendations for science and social studies. Every page reinforces a key concept in one of the subject areas. Your child will love the colorful art, familiar video game characters, and the fun approach to each learning activity!

The pages of this workbook are color coded to help you target specific skills areas as needed.

BLUE	Language Arts
ORANGE	Math
GREEN	Science
PINK	Social Studies

Whether it's the joy of seeing their favorite Minecraft characters on every page, the fun of solving a riddle or a puzzle, or the pride of accomplishment of completing a learning challenge, there is something in this book for even the most reluctant learner.

Happy adventuring!

CONTENTS

4

WORD JUMBLE

Write the words in the correct order so that the sentence makes sense. Don't forget to capitalize the first word in the sentence and add a period at the end.

1. a profession with Nitwit is no villager

_____

_____

2. used fish are fishing tools to catch rods

_____

_____

3. the job of the Ender Dragon is the Ender crystal to heal

_____

_____

4. the zombie pit fell into it and a player built the lava

_____

_____

READING WORDS

Draw a line to match each word to the picture.

1. anvil

A.

2. potion

B.

3. cauldron

C.

4. guardian

D.

5. obsidian

E.

6. piston

F.

RHYMING WORDS

Use the rhyming words to complete the sentences. Don't forget to capitalize the first word in the sentence.

bee	cow	ditch	gears	habit	pen
plow	rabbit	shears	ten	tree	witch

1. The _____ built its hive in a _____.

2. _____ pigs were in the _____.

3. The _____ pulled a _____ through the wheat field.

4. The _____ had a _____ of twitching its nose.

5. Steve cut the _____ with the _____.

6. The _____ used a pickaxe to build a _____ around its house.

I can make it **dis**appear!

PREFIXES

Draw a line from the prefix to a base word and write the new word on the line. Hint: Use each prefix and base word only once.

Prefix	Base Word	New Word
1. un	possible	
2. re	view	
3. pre	behave	
4. im	agree	
5. mis	school	
6. dis	seen	

PREFIXES

Add a prefix to each bolded base word to form a new word that fits the definition.

*I am **un**happy.*

Prefixes		
re – again	dis – opposite of	mis – incorrect
un – not	under – below	pre – before

Word | **Definition**

1. _____ to **view** again

2. _____ below **water**

3. _____ **spell** incorrectly

4. _____ **heat** before

5. _____ not **happy**

6. _____ opposite of **agree**

SUFFIXES

Add suffixes to the base words to form new words. Write the words under the suffix. The first one is done for you.

Bat is creep**y**.

excite	friend	dirt	child	care
wind	agree	noise	kind	retire	like

1.   -ment

excitement

agreement

retirement

2.   -y

3.   -ish

4.   -ness

5.   -ly

6.   -ship

SUFFIXES

Use the spelling rules to add the suffix to the base word.

Skeleton is run**ning**.

If a word ends in a short vowel and consonant, double the consonant before adding the suffix.	run ➤	running
If a word ends in a silent e, drop the e before adding the suffix.	hope ➤	hoping
If a word ends with a consonant y, change the y to i before adding the suffix.	happy ➤	happiness
If a word ends with a vowel y, just add the suffix.	joy ➤	joyful

1. hug + ing _____

2. jump + ed _____

3. slip + ed _____

4. slide + ing _____

5. hop + ing _____

6. dig + ing _____

7. beauty + ful _____

8. smile + ed _____

9. care + ing _____

10. cut + ing _____

PREFIXES AND SUFFIXES

Underline the prefix and circle the suffix in each word. Draw a line from the word to its meaning.

1. unforgettable

A. not able to be described

2. indescribable

B. not like a friend

3. misspelling

C. not full of help

4. unfriendly

D. not able to be controlled

5. unhelpful

E. not able to forget

6. uncontrollable

F. incorrect spelling

DIVIDING SYLLABLES

Draw a line between the syllables of each word. The first one is done for you.

Rules for Dividing Syllables

Divide between compound words	book/shelf
Divide between two consonant letters	zom/bie
Prefixes and suffixes are syllables	creep/er
Divide after the long vowel	ro/bot
Divide after the consonant following a short vowel	Al/ex

1. black/smith

2. dancing

3. zombie

4. villager

5. butterfly

6. cobweb

7. emeralds

8. Enderman

LEARNING NEW WORDS

Read the clues. Answer the questions.

1. In the real world, **elytra** are the wings of a beetle. In

Minecraft, elytra help the players do what?

A. attack   B. fly

2. In the real world, **diorite** is a speckled rock. In Minecraft,

a diorite block is used for what?

A. to make granite   B. for food

3. In the real world, a **portal** is a doorway or entrance.

In Minecraft, the Nether portal is used as what?

A. a gateway between the Overworld and the Nether

B. a boat to travel on water

4. In the real world, a **default** is given by the computer.

In Minecraft, who is a default player?

A. Steve   B. Creeper

5. In the real world, a **piston** moves fluid in an engine.

In Minecraft a piston does what?

A. grinds up other blocks   B. moves other blocks

DETERMINE MEANING OF WORDS

I love to learn new words!

Read the sentences. Use the context clues to determine the meaning of the underlined words. Circle the best meaning.

1. Steve and Alex thought the joke was so <u>hilarious</u> that they couldn't stop laughing.

   A. rude   B. funny

2. Steve had <u>insufficient</u> diamond blocks, so he could not make a sword.

   A. not enough   B. too many

3. Iron golem will not <u>permit</u> Evoker into a village.

   A. let or allow   B. protect or keep out

4. Creeper became <u>outraged</u> and exploded on the player.

   A. happy   B. angry

5. The Arctic Biome is <u>barren</u>, with few plants and animals.

   A. without life   B. with lots of life

DICTIONARY GUIDEWORDS

Read the guidewords at the top of each page. Then write the words in the box on the correct page.

Guidewords are the two words at the top of each dictionary page. All the words on the page of a dictionary come between the two words alphabetically.

potato	goat	bread	moon	flower	lava	carrot	butterfly
iron	apple	clock	magma	ocelot	emerald	lever	orb

1.

anvil   cat

_____

_____

_____

_____

2.

chicken   hug

_____

_____

_____

_____

3.

ink   melon

_____

_____

_____

_____

4.

minecart   rabbit

_____

_____

_____

_____

MULTIPLE MEANING WORDS

Read the sentence. Then circle the letter of the meaning that matches the underlined word.

1. The chickens were making a <u>racket</u>.
   A. a type of bat   B. a loud noise

2. The creeper will <u>charge</u> at the player.
   A. the cost of something   B. attack

3. The parrot's <u>bill</u> is black.
   A. an amount of money owed   B. the beak of a bird

4. The sunken <u>ship</u> was at the bottom of the ocean.
   A. a large boat   B. to send a package

5. Alex is trying to <u>train</u> pig.
   A. to teach   B. railroad cars

6. You can <u>change</u> the skins on your player.
   A. to make different   B. coins

HOMOPHONES

Read each sentence. Write the homophones on the lines to complete the sentence in a way that makes sense.

Homophones are words that sound the same but are spelled differently and have different meanings.

1. Horse _____ _____ carrots.   eight/ate

2. When cows _____ a creeper and   meat/meet

die, they drop _____ .

3. Steve _____ how to find the   new/knew

_____ entrance to the cave.

4. Creepers _____ that _____   know/no

mob can survive their explosion.

5. Creepers will drop _____ heads over   their/they're/there

_____ when _____ dying.

6. Those _____ creepers are _____   two/to/too

tired _____ play.

MORE HOMOPHONES

Circle the homophones in the puzzle.

Which witch?

blew/blue	whole/hole	weight/wait	road/rode	sea/see
peace/piece	knight/night	break/brake	wood/would	tale/tail

```
K N I G H T Z Y E R S N R W
N E T H G I E W C L O E D T
J B U Y J L R W A L O A A D
N G R L I Y D H E Y D H D Q
K T B A B R N O P P R T V R
M A T K K Z T L P E H E E S
D J E W Y E X E C G B W R J
R R N R X R L E I W E O Z T
W A I T B L I N O L D Q J T
D E J R T P T U B E Y L T N
O J L V D V L V Z Q M R T L
O K R A K D D B D R B X V D
W Q V J T J L T N G Y K B N
```

ON THE FARM

Read about Steve's adventure on the farm. Write the nouns on the lines. Circle all the proper nouns.

Nouns name people, places, things, or events. A **proper noun** names a one-of-a-kind noun. Proper nouns always begin with a capital letter.

Steve enjoys being on the farm. He likes to feed the animals. He likes to breed them too. The cows and sheep like to eat wheat. The pigs like to eat carrots or beetroots. The chickens like to eat seeds. Two animals will have a baby. Babies grow up in 20 minutes. Steve has to build lots of pens to keep the animals safe. He also builds a barn and a coop.

_____   _____

_____   _____

_____   _____

_____   _____

_____   _____

_____   _____

_____   _____

_____   _____

CREEPER ACTION

Choose a verb to complete each sentence. Write the verb in its correct form.

Verbs

run	explode	hiss	flash	attack	climb

1. Creeper _____ loudly when it saw the player.

2. Creeper will _____ any player within 16 blocks.

3. When creeper attacks, it _____.

4. Creeper can _____ ladders and vines.

5. Creeper _____ away from ocelots and cats.

6. Creeper _____ before it explodes.

ORDERING ADJECTIVES

Write adjectives on the lines to describe each picture. Use each adjective only once.

Adjectives

white	pink	yellow	green	five
creepy	long	cute	spotted	old

1. Ocelot is a _____ _____ cat.

2. Chicken laid _____ _____ eggs.

3. Nitwit wears _____ _____ clothing.

4. The _____ _____ house was haunted.

5. Alex tamed the _____ _____ pig.

ADVERBS

Underline the verb in the sentence once and the adverb twice. The first one is done for you.

An **adverb** describes an action verb. It tells how, when, or where and action happens.

1. Creeper <u>hissed</u> <u><u>loudly</u></u>.

2. Iron golem awkwardly handed the flower to the villager.

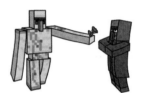

3. Alex gently cared for the animals.

4. The baby zombie villagers played happily.

5. Alex carefully put the diamond armor in the chest.

6. The bee buzzed quickly from flower to flower.

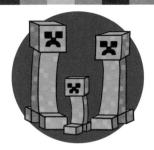

CONJUNCTIONS

Write the conjunction that best completes the sentence.

Conjunctions

and	or	but	so

1. Bees _____ bats have wings.

2. Chickens can swim, _____ baby chickens cannot.

3. Is that a shulker _____ a purpur block?

4. Witches can drink _____ throw potions.

5. Blaze is a fiery mob _____ be careful not to get burned.

6. A donkey can be controlled_____ first it must be tamed.

PREPOSITIONS

Complete each sentence using the correct preposition.

Prepositions

on	in	around	under	behind	over

1. The diamond armor is _____ the chest.

2. Steve is _____ the cow.

3. The carrot is _____ the stick.

4. The creepers are dancing _____ the disco ball.

5. Alex's arm is _____ cow.

6. Bat flew _____ the tree.

PREPOSITIONAL PHRASES

Circle the preposition and underline the prepositional phrase in each sentence. The first one is done for you.

1. Steve collected wood (from) the forest to build a shelter.

2. Steve climbed up a tree to get away from the mobs.

3. You can find a witch hut in the Swampland Biome.

4. Inside the witch hut, you can find a crafting table.

5. Horses can be found in the Plains Biome.

6. If you click on a horse, you can ride it.

PARTS OF A SENTENCE

Underline the subject once and the predicate twice. The first one is done for you.

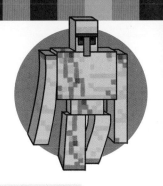

> The **subject** of a sentence tells who or what the sentence is about.
>
> The **predicate** of a sentence tells what the subject is or does.

1. The Minecraft world has many mobs.

2. You can tame some mobs.

3. Some mobs can be eaten.

4. Creeper likes to screech and explode.

5. Utility mobs can help a player.

6. Iron golem is a utility mob.

FRAGMENTS AND SENTENCES

*Write **S** if the group of words is a sentence. Write **F** if the group of words is a fragment.*

A **sentence** has a subject and a predicate.

A **fragment** is missing a subject or a predicate.

1. A passive mob will never attack a player. _____

2. A neutral mob like wolves and spiders. _____

3. Snow golem and iron golem are utility mobs. _____

4. An aggressive mob will attack on sight. _____

5. Looking to kill players. _____

6. Fun to interact with in the Minecraft world. _____

COMPOUND SENTENCES

Use a comma and a coordinating conjunction to combine the two sentences into one compound sentence. The first one is done for you.

Coordinating Conjunctions

and	or	but	so

1. Steve found a diamond. He put it in his cart.

Steve found a diamond, so he put it in his cart.

2. Steve wanted to tame a creeper. It exploded.

_____

3. Steve can go to the Desert Biome. He can go to the Jungle Biome.

_____

4. Steve likes to play in the village. Alex likes to play on the farm.

_____

PUNCTUATION AND CAPITALIZATION

Write each sentence on the line, adding capitals and punctuation.

1. zombies are undead hostile mobs

_____

2. watch out for baby zombies

_____

3. baby zombies are even more dangerous than big zombies

_____

4. on halloween, zombies put pumpkins on their heads

_____

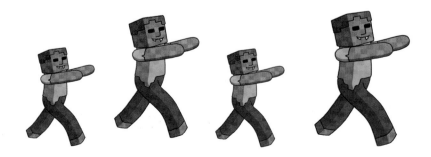

EDITING

Steve wrote a report about the venomous cave spider.
Use the editing marks to correct the mistakes.

     ∧   insert word

     ⎯ℓ   delete word

     ⊙   add period

     ⋏   insert comma

  sp.◯   correct spelling

     ≡   capitalize

Cave Spiders

Cave spiders live abandoned mineshafts they climb walls

and hid in cobwebs. The all so swim so very fast. They spawn frum

monster spawners They attak by jumping at there target. They are

very poisonous. When killed they can drop string or spider eye.

Busy as a bee.

ANIMAL SIMILES

Write the animal name that completes the simile.

A **simile** makes a comparison using *like* or *as*.

| mule | fox | bird | bunny | dog | bat | cat | horse |

1. free as a _____

2. blind as a _____

3. sick as a _____

4. hungry as a _____

5. stubborn as a _____

6. quick as a _____

7. curious as a _____

8. sly as a _____

MINECRAFT METAPHORS

Draw a line from the bolded metaphor to its meaning.

Don't be a chicken!

> A **metaphor** describes something by comparing it to something else.

1. Steve was **a volcano ready to explode.**

A. very quickly

2. Nitwit is **a funny duck.**

B. really tall

3. Zombie ran **lightning fast.**

C. really angry

4. Iron golem is **a giant.**

D. sounds lovely

5. Bird is **music to Steve's ears.**

E. silly

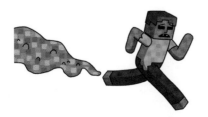

IDIOMS

Circle the best meaning of the bolded idioms.

An **idiom** is a saying that has a different meaning from its literal meaning.

1. Steve mined **until the cows came home.**

A. He kept mining until the cows were in the pen.

B. He kept mining for a long time.

2. Alex found a diamond in the mine that **knocked her socks off.**

A. The diamond was better than Alex expected.

B. The diamond made Alex's sock fall off.

3. Steve wasn't afraid of dog because he **knew its bark was worse than its bite.**

A. The dog liked to bark a lot.

B. The dog was loud, but not dangerous.

4. When Alex met the baby mooshroom, she thought **the apple doesn't fall far from the tree.**

A. Alex thought the baby mooshroom looked just like its parent.

B. Alex thought the baby mooshroom was hungry and would like to eat an apple.

5. When Steve saw Creeper explode, he was **waiting for the other shoe to drop.**

A. Creeper's explosion caused Steve's shoes to fly up in the air.

B. Steve was waiting for something else to go wrong.

6. Alex and Steve were **laughing their heads off.**

A. They laughed so hard their block heads came off.

B. They laughed hard.

MORE IDIOMS

Circle the best meaning of the bolded idioms.

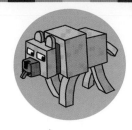

1. Alex was **over the moon** about her mobs.

A. Alex loved her mobs.
B. Alex went into space.

2. The villager gave witch **the cold shoulder.**

A. The villager ignored witch.
B. The villager hugged witch.

3. When Alex rode pig, **it was all ears.**

A. Pig had very large ears.
B. Pig listened to Alex.

4. The potion cost Wither an **arm and a leg.**

A. Wither lost its arms and legs when it drank the potion.
B. The potion cost Wither a lot.

5. Steve **drew a blank** during his math test.

A. Steve couldn't remember how to do the problem.
B. Steve drew a blank square on his math test.

6. Steve **called it a day** after exploring for hours.

A. Steve thought exploring should be called a day.
B. Steve quit exploring for the day.

WRITE A STORY

Use the characters, items, and setting pictured to write a story. Before writing, use the graphic organizer to plan your story.

Characters and Items

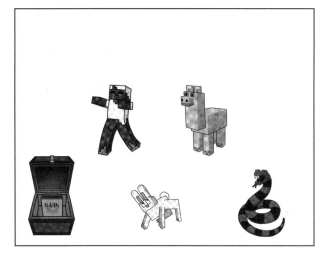

Setting

What is the problem to be solved?

Beginning or Introduction

Middle or Action

Ending or Solution

WRITE A STORY

_____

_____

_____

_____

_____

_____

_____

_____

_____

_____

_____

WRITE AN OPINION

Do you think playing Minecraft is a good activity for kids? Write your opinion. Use the graphic organizer to plan your writing.

Your Opinion

Reason 1	Reason 2	Reason 3

Examples/evidence: Examples/evidence: Examples/evidence:

_____   _____   _____

_____   _____   _____

_____   _____   _____

_____   _____   _____

Your Conclusion

WRITE AN OPINION

_____

_____

_____

_____

_____

_____

_____

_____

_____

_____

_____

WRITE TO INFORM

Write to inform a new player something about Minecraft. Use the graphic organizer to plan your informational writing.

Topic: _____

_____

Topic Sentence: _____

_____

_____

Fact 1	Fact 2	Fact 3

Concluding Sentence:

_____

_____

_____

WRITE TO INFORM

_____

_____

_____

_____

_____

_____

_____

_____

_____

_____

_____

SEQUENCING EVENTS

Read how to craft a beacon. Write the steps in the correct order.

How to Craft a Beacon

Beacons are useful for creating light. They shine a light beam toward the sky. They also can melt snow and ice. In addition, they can give players status effects. To make a beacon you will need a crafting table, five glass blocks, three obsidian blocks, and a nether star. Place the three obsidian blocks along the bottom row of the crafting table. Place the nether star in the center of the table. Fill the rest of the table with the glass blocks. Set the beacon on a pyramid to activate it.

Steps to Crafting a Beacon

1. Get _____

2. Place _____

3. Place _____

4. Place _____

5. Set _____

LOGICAL THINKING

Read the clues to craft a Minecraft cake. Draw the ingredients on the crafting board.

Recipe for Cake

3 wheat    1 egg

2 sugar    3 milk

To make a cake you will need a
3 x 3 crafting board.

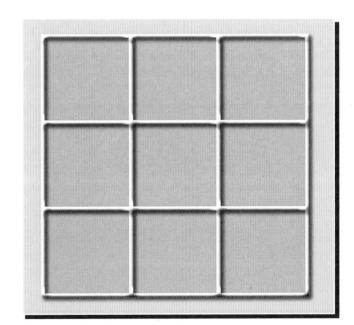

➡ Place the egg in the center.

➡ Place all the wheat on the same row.

➡ Place all the milk on the same row.

➡ Place the milk above the egg.

➡ Place the sugar.

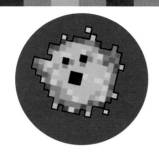

CAUSE AND EFFECT

Draw a line to match the cause with the effect.

Cause is the why something happens.

Effect is what happens.

1. If you press "use" on a donkey,

2. If a player finds a bat hanging upside-down,

3. If you have a monster spawner,

4. If a player eats a pufferfish,

5. If you kill a chicken,

A. the player will die.

B. it drops a feather.

C. it will screech and fly away.

D. a chest is added so it can carry things.

E. you can spawn mobs.

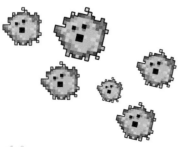

CAUSE AND EFFECT

Complete the missing parts of the chart to show cause and effect.

Cause	Effect
1. If you want to get metal from a block,	
2.	right click on a villager.
3. Because ocelots are passive, shy mobs,	
4.	you will need a saddle.
5. If you have a cooked rabbit, a carrot, a baked potato, a mushroom, and a bowl,	
6.	a skeleton will shoot arrows.

COMPARE AND CONTRAST

Compare and contrast two different villagers.

Compare means to tell how two or more things are alike.

Contrast means to tell how two or more things are different.

Villager 1

_____

Color of clothing: _____

Job: _____

Where it lives: _____

Passive or hostile? (circle one)

Villager 2

_____

Color of clothing: _____

Job: _____

Where it lives: _____

Passive or hostile? (circle one)

How are the villagers alike?

How are the villagers different?

ROUNDING NUMBERS

Round the numbers to the nearest 10.

We don't do a lot of rounding in Minecraft.

Rounding Rules

If the ones digit is less than 5, round the number **down** to the nearest 10.

If the ones digit is 5 or more, round the number **up** to the nearest 10.

1. 57 ➜ _____

2. 65 ➜ _____

3. 33 ➜ _____

4. 17 ➜ _____

5. 94 ➜ _____

6. 23 ➜ _____

7. 83 ➜ _____

8. 15 ➜ _____

9. 99 ➜ _____

10. 6 ➜ _____

11. 71 ➜ _____

12. 52 ➜ _____

13. 68 ➜ _____

14. 25 ➜ _____

15. 39 ➜ _____

16. 42 ➜ _____

17. 13 ➜ _____

18. 70 ➜ _____

NUMBERS TO 9999

Use place value to write the missing numbers in the blocks.

1. 6,725 = 6,000 + ⬡ + 20 + ⬡

2. 1,489 = ⬡ + ⬡ + 80 + 9

3. 8,046 = 8,000 + ⬡ + 6

4. 9,999 = 9,000 + 900 + ⬡ + ⬡

5. 4,391 = ⬡ + 300 + 90 + ⬡

6. 2,814 = ⬡ + 800 + ⬡ + 4

7. 3,729 = 3,000 + 700 + ⬡ + ⬡

8. 5,602 = 5,000 + ⬡ + 2

9. 7,947 = 7,000 + ⬡ + 40 + ⬡

COMPARING NUMBERS TO 9999

Use <, >, or = to compare the numbers.

1. 3,466 ☐ 3,456

2. 7,817 ☐ 7,871

3. 4,543 ☐ 5,543

4. 2,727 ☐ 2,772

5. 7,089 ☐ 7,809

6. 8,369 ☐ 8,371

7. 4,004 ☐ 3,899

8. 6,009 ☐ 6,010

9. 9,917 ☐ 9,917

10. 1,008 ☐ 998

11. 2,801 ☐ 2,108

12. 4,732 ☐ 4,702

ADDITION

Solve the problems. Complete the puzzle.

ACROSS

1 2,753 + 697

2 1,472 + 1,509

4 5,931 + 3,300

7 1,999 + 2,532

11 311 + 107

12 254 + 348

13 87 + 118

14 465 + 273

15 137 + 326

16 309 + 204

DOWN

1 1,340 + 1,936

3 1,080 + 302

4 7,816 + 1,608

5 1,497 + 609

6 1,319 + 2,534

8 2,798 + 2,877

9 3,000 + 31

10 814 + 469

ADDITION

Solve each problem. Use the answers to solve the riddle.

1. 631
  + 227

2. 525
  + 132

3. 733
  + 126

R

T

H

4. 171
  + 268

5. 142
  + 351

6. 483
  + 310

F

O

S

7. 253
  + 373

8. 338
  + 541

9. 654
  + 215

L

E

I

Q: What is the last thing that Steve takes off before going to bed?

COPY THE LETTERS FROM THE ANSWERS ABOVE TO FIND OUT.

859 869 793   439 879 879 657   493 439 439

657 859 879   439 626 493 493 858

SUBTRACTION
Solve the problems. Complete the puzzle.

ACROSS

2 7,304 – 4992

4 4,742 – 4,715

DOWN

1 2,340 – 2,293

3 5,107 – 2,303

4 8,001 – 7,766

5 7,719 – 3,359

6 6,847 – 1640

7 9,843 – 5,982

8 6,874 – 831

9 7,100 – 6794

10 611 – 426

11 4,604 – 3,663

12 3,999 – 3,764

SUBTRACTION

Solve each problem. Use the answers to solve the riddle.

C - O - W

1. 426
  - 125

  D

2. 325
  - 172

  L

3. 513
  - 282

  H

4. 671
  - 168

  Y

5. 346
  - 201

  O

6. 483
  - 117

  S

7. 853
  - 326

  U

8. 738
  - 544

  E

9. 564
  - 215

  B

Q: How do you spell cow using fourteen letters?

COPY THE LETTERS FROM THE ANSWERS ABOVE TO FIND OUT.

366 194 194   145 231

301 145 527 349 153 194   503 145 527

NUMBER PUZZLES

Complete the number puzzles using the numbers 1, 2, 3, 4, 5, and 6, so that each line (across and up and down) equals the number in the block.

1.

2
1

11

2.

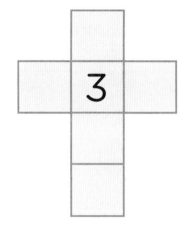

3

12

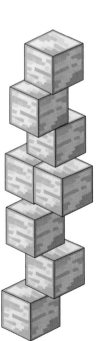

3.

5

13

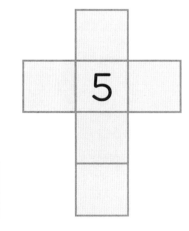

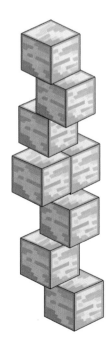

PROBLEM SOLVING IN THE ARCTIC

Read and solve each problem. Use the box to show how you solved the problem.

1. The Arctic Biome is home to 234 polar bears and 366 white rabbits. How many of these animals live in the Arctic Biome?

_____

2. There were 431 fish in the ocean surrounding the arctic biome. The polar bears ate 179 fish. How many fish were left?

_____

3. Steve spotted 327 adult polar bears. He said that there were 132 fewer baby polar bears than adult polar bears. How many baby polar bears did he see?

_____

4. Steve walked many steps across the frozen tundra of the Arctic Biome. He walked 523 steps the first day and 488 steps the second day. How many steps did he walk all together?

_____

SUMS AND PRODUCTS

Add the numbers to get the sum. Multiply the numbers to get the product. The first one is done for you.

1.
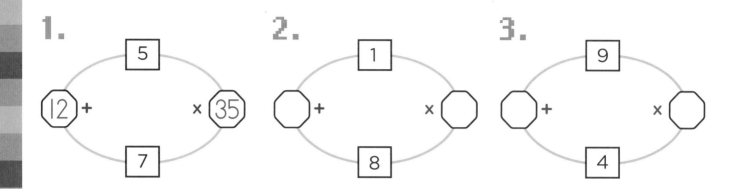

5
(12) + × (35)
7

2.

1
◯ + × ◯
8

3.

9
◯ + × ◯
4

4.
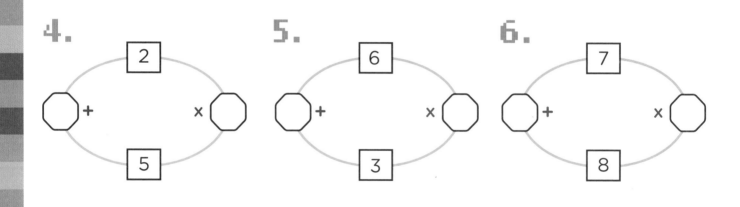

2
◯ + × ◯
5

5.

6
◯ + × ◯
3

6.

7
◯ + × ◯
8

7.
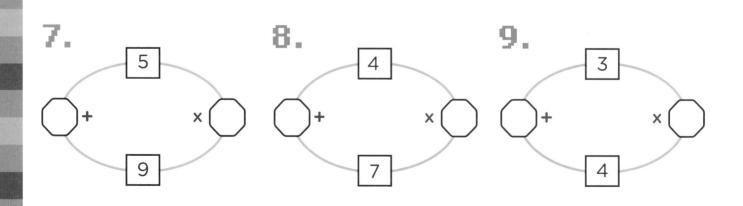

5
◯ + × ◯
9

8.

4
◯ + × ◯
7

9.

3
◯ + × ◯
4

MULTIPLICATION FACTS

Multiply the numbers by the center number. The first one is done for you.

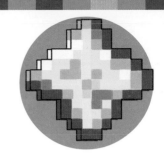

1.

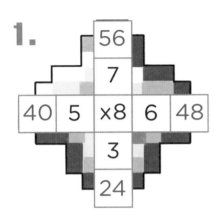

56
7
40 5 ×8 6 48
3
24

2.

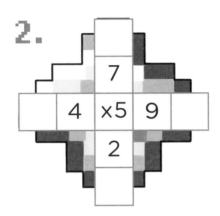

7
4 ×5 9
2

3.

3
9 ×2 4
7

4.

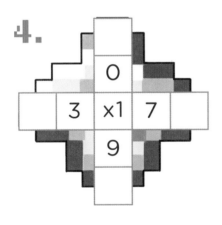

0
3 ×1 7
9

5.

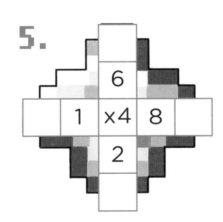

6
1 ×4 8
2

6.

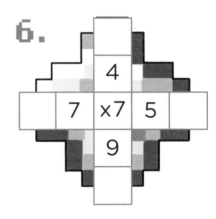

4
7 ×7 5
9

7.

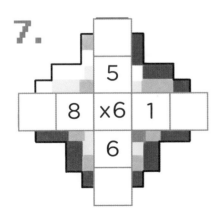

5
8 ×6 1
6

8.

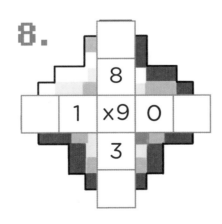

8
1 ×9 0
3

9.

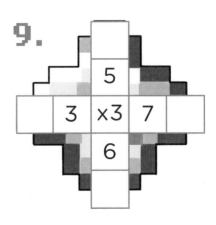

5
3 ×3 7
6

FACTORS

Draw a line to match the factor pairs. Cross out any numbers that are not factors. The first one is done for you.

Factors are the numbers that can be multiplied together to get a product.

The factors of 4 are 1, 2, and 4. $1 \times 4 = 4$ $2 \times 2 = 4$

1. Factors of 20

1   10   4   ~~6~~

5   ~~3~~   2   20

2. Factors of 12

6   7   12   3

1   4   2   8

3. Factors of 24

24   6   3   2

8   12   4   1

4. Factors of 36

9   6   2   12   1

36   6   3   4   18

5. Factors of 42

7   8   42   3   2

21   9   6   1   14

6. Factors of 25

9   1   7   5

9   5   2   25

7. Factors of 27

27   7   4   9

2   3   1   6

8. Factors of 35

5   3   15   1

35   4   10   7

9. Factors of 48

6   3   48   12   2

24   4   8   1   16

FACTORS

Write the factor pairs on chicken's eggs.

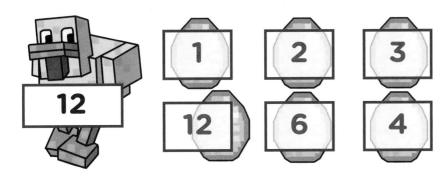

12

| 1 | 2 | 3 |
| 12 | 6 | 4 |

1.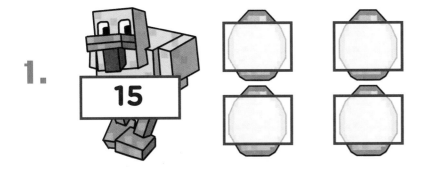

15

2.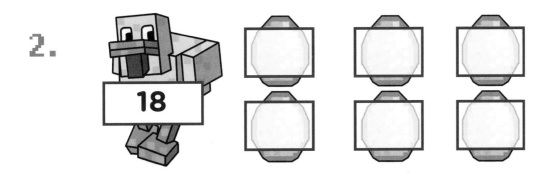

18

3.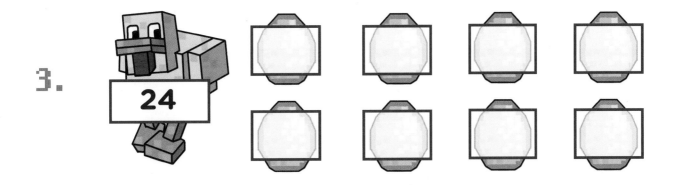

24

MULTIPLES

Color the multiples to help Zombie find his way safely around the lava.

1. multiples of 3

START →

3	6	13	4	7	9	43	31	6	8
1	9	15	2	21	5	20	22	10	98
17	53	19	18	35	24	29	40	2	11
46	83	16	26	13	23	27	28	71	62
89	44	95	47	52	65	38	30	70	57
20	78	55	88	14	67	86	33	51	49
59	74	14	42	93	73	77	36	39	68
12	52	22	61	50	25	80	23	37	42

END

2. multiples of 4

START →

4	8	7	16	14	13	6	19	9	21
30	5	12	2	20	19	27	22	1	42
64	3	10	15	24	35	33	51	17	32
58	14	29	70	28	34	78	53	49	45
90	37	47	32	6	73	86	94	99	50
83	74	43	69	36	11	57	2	25	63
81	39	12	77	51	40	44	48	18	17
61	34	95	76	22	55	66	82	52	56

END

MORE MULTIPLES

Color the multiples to help Zombie find his way safely around the lava.

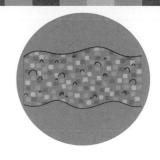

1. multiples of 5

START →

5	12	17	21	2	6	19	27	11	8
10	15	24	22	3	9	18	1	7	16
14	13	20	27	30	35	28	33	29	31
72	61	59	25	53	46	40	47	39	37
88	84	66	78	91	94	45	56	58	62
97	92	83	79	69	89	74	50	99	78
28	36	49	52	80	19	83	55	73	81
77	54	48	37	61	93	76	60	65	70

END

2. multiples of 9

START →

9	18	32	11	31	7	49	8	18	21
1	2	27	3	6	67	19	20	47	36
14	39	40	36	45	10	4	9	5	12
38	29	25	17	54	44	76	13	55	53
50	89	82	15	60	63	98	73	69	70
62	12	28	97	85	79	72	81	37	64
49	21	46	95	23	77	86	66	90	83
84	13	67	30	52	88	80	57	42	99

END

Cool pattern!

MULTIPLYING BY TENS

Multiply by tens.

Hint: 3 x 7 = 21   3 x 70 = 210   30 x 70 = 2,100

1. 5 x 9 = _____   **2.** 50 x 9 = _____   **3.** 5 x 90 = _____   **4.** 50 x 90 = _____

5. 8 x 3 = _____   **6.** 8 x 30 = _____   **7.** 80 x 3 = _____   **8.** 80 x 30 = _____

9. 7 x 6 = _____   **10.** 7 x 60 = _____   **11.** 70 x 6 = _____   **12.** 70 x 60 = _____

13. 1 x 4 = _____   **14.** 10 x 4 = _____   **15.** 1 x 40 = _____   **16.** 10 x 40 = _____

17. 9 x 2 = _____   **18.** 90 x 2 = _____   **19.** 9 x 20 = _____   **20.** 90 x 20 = _____

21. 7 x 5 = _____   **22.** 7 x 50 = _____   **23.** 0 x 5 = _____   **24.** 70 x 50 = _____

25. 6 x 8 = _____   **26.** 60 x 8 = _____   **27.** 6 x 80 = _____   **28.** 60 x 80 = _____

29. 3 x 4 = _____   **30.** 30 x 4 = _____   **31.** 3 x 40 = _____   **32.** 30 x 40 = _____

MULTIPLYING BY 10, 100, 1,000

Multiply to complete the chart.

I feel like a genius with multiplying by 10, 100, and 1,000.

Write the answers to the multiplication problems, such as 24 X 10, in the spaces.

	x10	x100	x1,000
1. 24			
2. 15			
3. 27			
4. 36			
5. 42			
6. 61			
7. 58			
8. 73			
9. 86			
10. 90			

MULTIPLYING

Find the product of each problem. Then use the key to color.

less than 1,000	1,000 – 1,999	2,000 – 2,999	3,000 – 3,999	4,000 and over	

				23 x45			
			56 x16	33 x21	29 x19		
			49 x17	59 x16	15 x47		
	65 x61		64 x29	22 x44	37 x38		
		82 x40	11 x36	85 x62	18 x42	72 x54	
			98 x45	77 x69	61 x88	58 x58	
				59 x68			
				64 x93		44 x52	
		35 x58		53 x79	49 x47		
			59 x42	99 x99			
				83 x78			
		95 x38		64 x87		86 x45	
78 x51	86 x95		24 x89	73 x92	33 x65		43 x77
	73 x54	70 x85	90 x44	35 x60	66 x89	36 x85	53 x48

64

MULTIPLYING

Solve each problem. Use the answers to solve the riddle.

1. 23
   x 27

2. 65
   x 32

3. 43
   x 46

4. 30
   x 25

A

5. 71
   x 68

T

6. 42
   x 51

N

7. 23
   x 31

H

8. 13
   x 52

G

9. 53
   x 33

O

10. 34
   x 42

W

11. 54
   x 15

D

12. 33
   x 44

B   I   Y   E

Q: Why didn't skeleton go to the party?

COPY THE LETTERS FROM THE ANSWERS ABOVE TO FIND OUT.

___ ____   ___   ___   ___   _____ _____ _____ _____ ___   ___
750 1,452 750   621   676   1,978 2,142 1,749 2,142 676   810

_____ _____   _____ _____   ___   _____ _____ ___
2,080 2,142   4,828 2,142   713   1,428 2,080 750

65

DIVISION FACTS

Solve the problems. Use the key to color the orb.

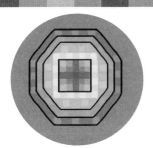

■	■	■	■	■	■	■
1	2	3	4	5,6	6,7	8,9

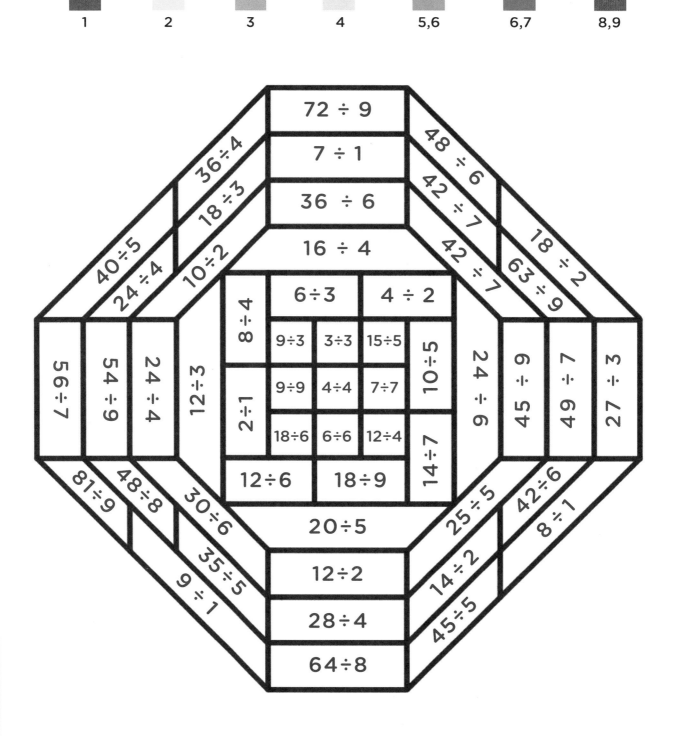

72 ÷ 9

36÷4

7 ÷ 1

48 ÷ 6

18÷3

36 ÷ 6

42 ÷ 7

40÷5

24 ÷ 4

10÷2

16 ÷ 4

42 ÷ 7

18 ÷ 2

63 ÷ 9

8÷4

6÷3

4 ÷ 2

9÷3 3÷3 15÷5

10÷5

56÷7

54÷9

24 ÷ 4

12÷3

2÷1

9÷9 4÷4 7÷7

24 ÷ 6

45 ÷ 9

49 ÷ 7

27 ÷ 3

18÷6 6÷6 12÷4

14÷7

12 ÷ 6

18 ÷ 9

81÷9

48÷8

30÷6

20÷5

25 ÷ 5

42÷6

8 ÷ 1

35÷5

12÷2

14 ÷ 2

9 ÷ 1

28 ÷ 4

45÷5

64÷8

DIVISION FACTS

Complete the missing numbers in the division equations.
The first one is done for you.

1.

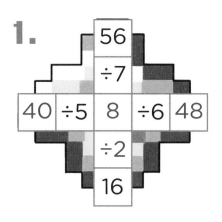

56
÷7
40 ÷5 8 ÷6 48
÷2
16

2.

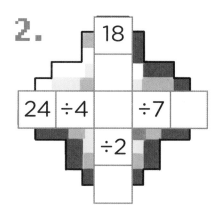

18
24 ÷4 ÷7
÷2

3.

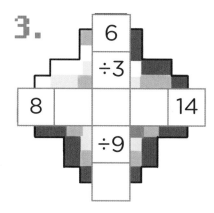

6
÷3
8 14
÷9

4.

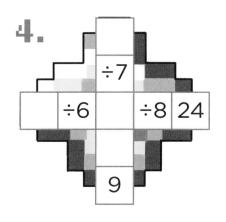

÷7
÷6 ÷8 24
9

5.

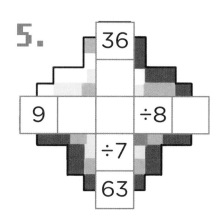

36
9 ÷8
÷7
63

6.

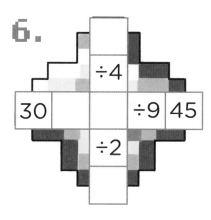

÷4
30 ÷9 45
÷2

7.

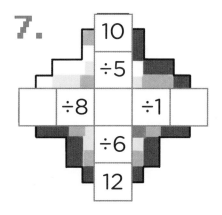

10
÷5
÷8 ÷1
÷6
12

8.

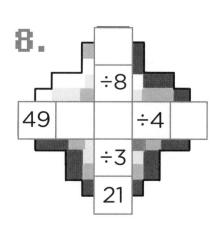

÷8
49 ÷4
÷3
21

9.

÷5
÷3 ÷6
÷2
8

DIVISION WITH REMAINDERS

Solve each problem. Use the answers to solve the riddle.

1. $3\overline{)29}$

2. $5\overline{)36}$

3. $7\overline{)48}$

4. $9\overline{)82}$

5. $8\overline{)20}$

A   C   E   L   O

6. $4\overline{)19}$

7. $6\overline{)57}$

8. $3\overline{)16}$

9. $2\overline{)17}$

10. $5\overline{)27}$

V   U   S   P   N

11. $8\overline{)46}$

12. $5\overline{)22}$

13. $7\overline{)29}$

14. $9\overline{)35}$

15. $3\overline{)20}$

T   G   H   I   D

Q: Why did pig spread a blanket on the ground?

COPY THE LETTERS FROM THE ANSWERS ABOVE TO FIND OUT.

5R1   2R4   3R8   5R6   7R1   2R4   9R3   9R1   6R2

4R1   9R2   4R3   6R6   9R2   8R1   3R8   4R2   5R2   3R8   7R1   .

DIVISION WITH REMAINDERS

Draw a line from the problem on Steve's minecart to the block that shows the answer.

1.  $58 \div 9$

A.  8R4

2.  $60 \div 7$

B.  5R6

3.  $37 \div 5$

C.  6R4

4.  $46 \div 8$

D.  7R2

5.  $27 \div 6$

E. 4R3

MOB'S MATH

Read and solve each problem. Use the box to show how you solved the problem.

1. 27 zombies spawned at the edge of the village. Each zombie spawned 3 baby zombies. How many zombies (adult and baby zombies) were there?

_____

2. There were 46 zombies and 9 monster spawners that the zombies shared equally. How many zombies used each of the monster spawners?

_____

3. Steve saw 19 creepers hiding behind the house and three times as many hiding in the forest. How many creepers did Steve see?

_____

4. There were 6 sand pits in the desert. 15 husks were trapped in each pit. How many husks were trapped in the sand pits?

_____

MOB'S MATH

Read and solve each problem. Use the box to show how you solved the problem.

1. 42 iron golems lived in the village. They each gave 3 flowers to the villagers. How many flowers were given away?

_____

2. The librarian stacked lots of books. He had 77 books and 6 shelves. How many books were on each shelf?

_____

3. Mooshrooms were spawning everywhere. There were 63 mooshrooms spawned in one week. How many mooshrooms were spawned each day?

_____

4. Nitwit was having trouble figuring out how many apples he has on his apple trees. He has 232 trees and 10 apples on each tree. How many apples does he have?

_____

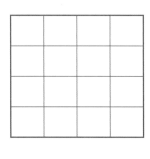

ORDERING FRACTIONS

Color to show each fraction. Then order the fractions from smallest to largest.

1.
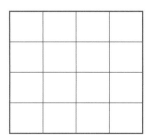

$$\frac{1}{2}$$

2.
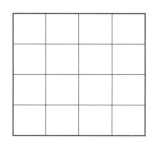

$$\frac{1}{4}$$

3.
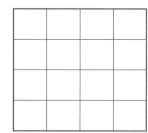

$$\frac{15}{16}$$

4.
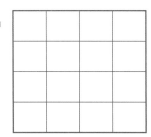

$$\frac{5}{8}$$

5.
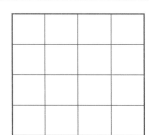

$$\frac{3}{4}$$

6.
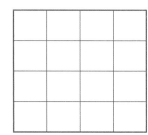

$$\frac{1}{16}$$

7.
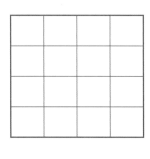

$$\frac{3}{16}$$

8.
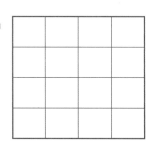

$$\frac{7}{8}$$

9.
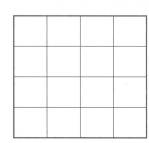

$$\frac{1}{8}$$

Write the fractions from smallest to largest.

____ ____ ____ ____ ____ ____ ____ ____ ____

EQUIVALENT FRACTIONS

Color to show each fraction. Draw a line to match the equivalent fractions.

These towers are equivalent.

1. $\dfrac{1}{2}$

A. $\dfrac{2}{6}$

2. $\dfrac{1}{3}$

B. $\dfrac{2}{8}$

3. $\dfrac{3}{4}$

C. $\dfrac{6}{10}$

4. $\dfrac{1}{4}$

D. $\dfrac{4}{8}$

5. $\dfrac{3}{5}$

E. $\dfrac{6}{8}$

ADDING FRACTIONS

Write each fraction, then add.

1.

+   =

_____   _____   _____

2.

+   =

_____   _____   _____

3.

+   =

_____   _____   _____

4.

+   =

_____   _____   _____

5.

+   =

_____   _____   _____

6.

+   =

_____   _____   _____

SUBTRACTING FRACTIONS

Subtract the fractions. Color to show the first fraction. Then cross out the second fraction. Write the fraction that remains.

1. $\dfrac{4}{9}$ − $\dfrac{1}{9}$ = $\dfrac{3}{9}$

2. $\dfrac{5}{8}$ − $\dfrac{4}{8}$ = _____

3. $\dfrac{3}{6}$ − $\dfrac{1}{6}$ = _____

4. $\dfrac{7}{9}$ − $\dfrac{2}{9}$ = _____

5. $\dfrac{4}{6}$ − $\dfrac{1}{6}$ = _____

6. $\dfrac{6}{8}$ − $\dfrac{4}{8}$ = _____

MULTIPLY FRACTIONS BY WHOLE NUMBERS

Multiply the fractions.

1.

3 x $\dfrac{1}{2}$ = $1\dfrac{1}{2}$

2.

2 x $\dfrac{1}{3}$ = _____

3.

4 x $\dfrac{1}{3}$ = _____

4.

4 x $\dfrac{1}{6}$ = _____

5.

5 x $\dfrac{1}{4}$ = _____

6.

2 x $\dfrac{1}{3}$ = _____

COOKING WITH WITCH

Read and solve each problem. Use the box to show how you solved the problem.

1. Witch needs $\frac{1}{2}$ cup sugar for the potion of swiftness. He wants to make 3 batches. How much sugar will he need all together?

   _____

2. Witch needs $\frac{1}{5}$ cup of blaze powder for one batch of potion of Strength and $\frac{3}{5}$ cup of blaze powder for another batch of potion of Strength. How much blaze powder does he need all together? _____

3. Witch found $\frac{2}{3}$ of a glistening melon in the front yard and $\frac{1}{3}$ of a glistening melon in the back yard. How much of a glistening melon did he have all together?

   _____

4. Witch had a cup of sugar. He needed $\frac{1}{4}$ of a cup to make a potion of Swiftness. How much sugar did he have left over?

   _____

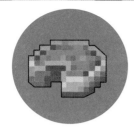

DECIMALS

Write each fraction as a decimal.

Decimals are another way to show fractions or numbers less than one.

$\frac{7}{10}$ = .7

$\frac{7}{100}$ = .07

$\frac{17}{100}$ = .17

1. $\frac{4}{10}$ = _____

2. $\frac{32}{100}$ = _____

3. $\frac{50}{100}$ = _____

4. $\frac{7}{10}$ = _____

5. $\frac{8}{100}$ = _____

6. $\frac{16}{100}$ = _____

7. $\frac{3}{100}$ = _____

8. $\frac{2}{10}$ = _____

9. $\frac{28}{100}$ = _____

10. $\frac{9}{100}$ = _____

Which number is the smallest?

_____

Which number is the largest?

_____

78

DECIMALS

Write the fraction and the decimal of each shaded part.

1.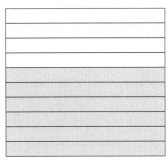

____ = . ____

2.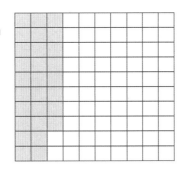

____ = . ____

3.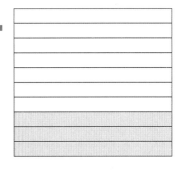

____ = . ____

4.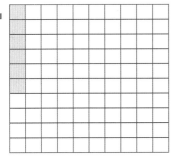

____ = . ____

5.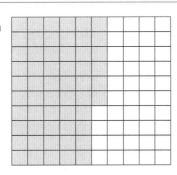

____ = . ____

6.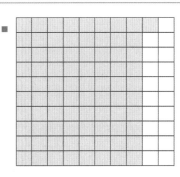

____ = . ____

7.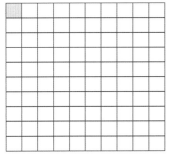

____ = . ____

8.

____ = . ____

9.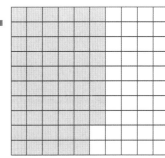

____ = . ____

STAIR PATTERNS

Look at the pyramid patterns. Complete the chart.
Draw the last stairs with 8 steps.

1 step = 1 block

2 steps = 3 blocks

3 steps = 6 blocks

4 steps = _____ blocks

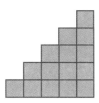

5 steps = _____ blocks

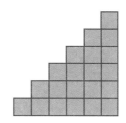

6 steps = _____ blocks

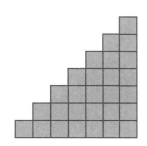

7 steps = _____ blocks

8 steps = _____ blocks

Steps	Number of blocks
1	1
2	3
3	6
4	
5	
6	
7	
8	

PYRAMID PATTERNS

Look at the pyramid patterns. Complete the chart.
Draw the fifth pyramid.

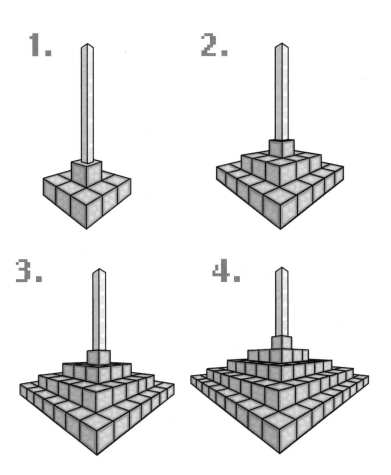

1.

2.

3.

4.

5.

Pyramid	Pyramid Base Size	Number of Blocks
1	3 x 3 = 9	9
2	5 x 5 = 25	34
3	7 x 7 =	
4	9 x 9 =	
5		

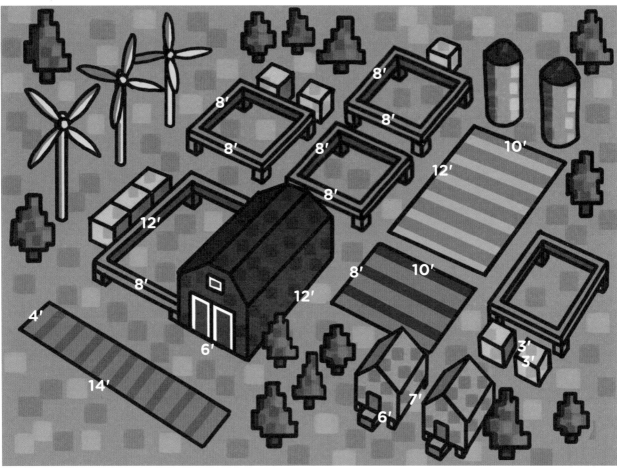

Perimeter is the distance around a shape.

Look at the measurements around the farm.
Write the perimeter of each.

1. barn _____

2. one chicken house _____

3. pen beside the barn _____

4. corn crop _____

5. one of the pens behind the barn _____

6. lettuce crop _____

7. one bale of hay _____

8. green pepper crop _____

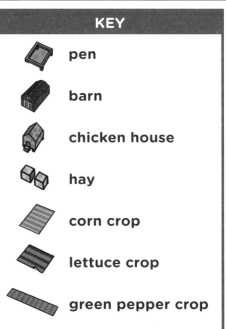

KEY
pen
barn
chicken house
hay
corn crop
lettuce crop
green pepper crop

AREA

Find the area of each square.

1.

_____ length

_____ width

_____ area

2.

_____ length

_____ width

_____ area

3.

_____ length

_____ width

_____ area

4.

_____ length

_____ width

_____ area

5.

_____ length

_____ width

_____ area

6.

_____ length

_____ width

_____ area

7. What pattern do you see in the numbers? This pattern is a formula for

finding the area of a rectangle. _____

_____

_____

Most angles in Minecraft are right angles.

ANGLES

Circle the word that describes each angle.

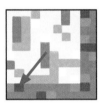

acute angle
less than 90°

right angle
90°

obtuse angle
greater than 90°

1.

acute   right   obtuse

2.

acute   right   obtuse

3.

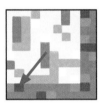

acute   right   obtuse

4.

acute   right   obtuse

5.

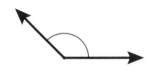

acute   right   obtuse

6.

acute   right   obtuse

7.

acute   right   obtuse

8.

acute   right   obtuse

9.

acute   right   obtuse

ANGLES

*Write **acute**, **obtuse**, or **right** to describe each angle.*

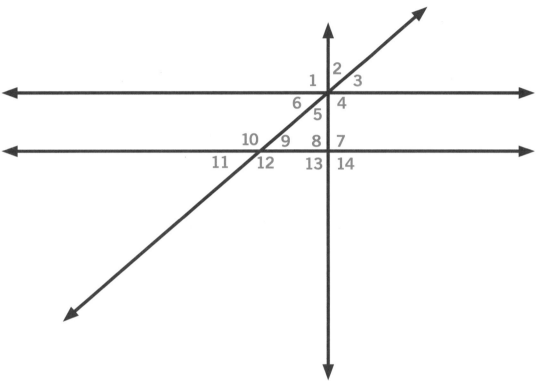

1. _____   8. _____

2. _____   9. _____

3. _____   10. _____

4. _____   11. _____

5. _____   12. _____

6. _____   13. _____

7. _____   14. _____

LINES

Lines are made up of points. Study the different types of lines in the chart. Answer the questions.

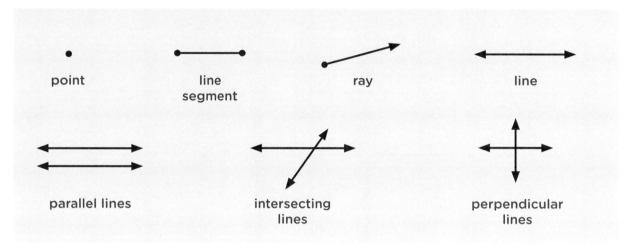

1. _____ lines never touch.

2. A _____ is shown with two arrows, meaning it goes on forever.

3. A _____ is a straight line between two points.

4. A _____ is a straight line that begins at a point and continues forever.

5. _____ lines cross each other.

6. A _____ is shown with a dot.

7. _____ lines touch or cross at right angles.

DRAWING WITH LINES

Follow the directions to create the line pictures.

1. Draw 10 rays shining from the sun.

2. Draw a track for Steve's minecart that includes 2 parallel line segments and 4 perpendicular line segments between the parallel line segments.

3. Draw another diamond sword that intersects with the sword pictured.

4. Connect the points (dots) to create snow golem.

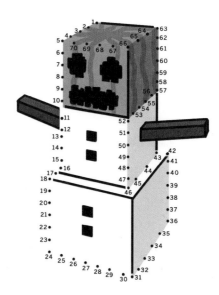

A square has two sets of parallel lines.

LINES AND SHAPES

Follow the directions to create or mark the lines.
The first one is done for you.

1. Make the line segments into lines.

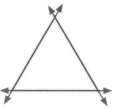

2. Color one set of parallel lines blue. Color the other set of parallel lines red.

3. Mark an X where the line segments intersect.

4. Color the perpendicular lines green.

5. Color one set of parallel lines blue. Color the other set of parallel lines red.

RESPIRATORY SYSTEM

My respiratory system helps me blow the dandelion!

Read about the respiratory system.
Label the parts.

The respiratory system makes it possible for us to take in fresh air and get rid of stale air. Air enters the body through the **nose** and **mouth**. Then the air moves through the **larynx** to the **trachea**. From the trachea, the air enters the **lungs**. We have two lungs. Both lungs have small tubes called the **bronchi**. The bronchi fill up with air and expand the lungs. The **diaphragm** is a muscle under the lungs. It helps the lungs fill with air. It also helps to push the air out of the lungs.

diaphragm	trachea	larynx	lungs
mouth	nose	bronchi	

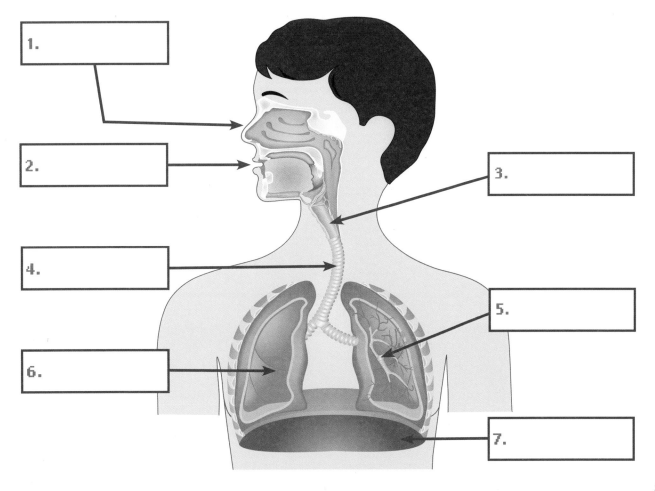

1.

2.

3.

4.

5.

6.

7.

Let's see how my body uses this cake.

DIGESTIVE SYSTEM

Read about the digestive system. Draw a line to trace the path that food travels through the body.

The digestive system changes food into energy. Food enters into the digestive system through the **mouth** where it is chewed. The food travels down the **esophagus** to the **stomach**. The stomach breaks down the food. Then the food enters the **small intestines**. The small intestines absorb the nutrients to make the body strong. The food then moves to the **large intestines**. The large intestines absorb water from the food. Food that is not used leaves the body through the **rectum**.

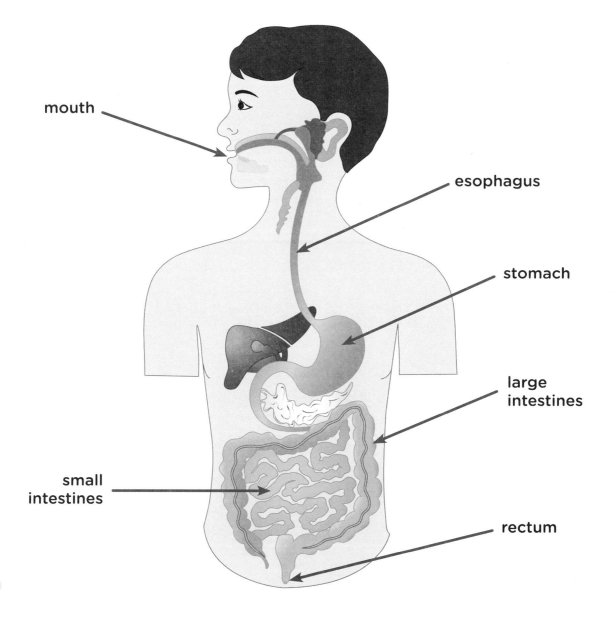

mouth

esophagus

stomach

large intestines

small intestines

rectum

CIRCULATORY SYSTEM

♥ means health.

Read about the circulatory system. Color the veins blue and the arteries red. Draw arrows to show how the blood moves through the body. Label the heart.

The circulatory system is the way the blood travels through the body. It is made up of muscles and organs. The heart is the most important muscle in our body. **Veins** carry blood toward the heart. **Arteries** carry the blood away from the heart. It takes the blood only a few seconds to travel through the whole body.

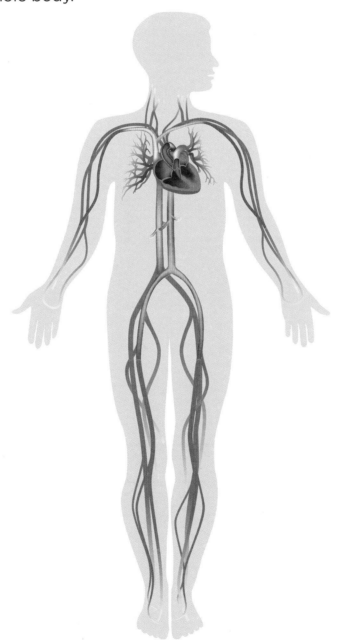

Maybe I need a nervous system.

NERVOUS SYSTEM

Read about the nervous system. Label the parts.

The nervous system is made up of the **brain**, **spinal cord**, and **nerves**. The brain is in the skull. It sends commands down the spinal cord and through the nerves to the different parts of the body. The brain tells the muscles when and how to move. It controls the heart's beating and the lungs' breathing. The brain's job is to protect the body. Taking a deep breath is one way to calm the brain.

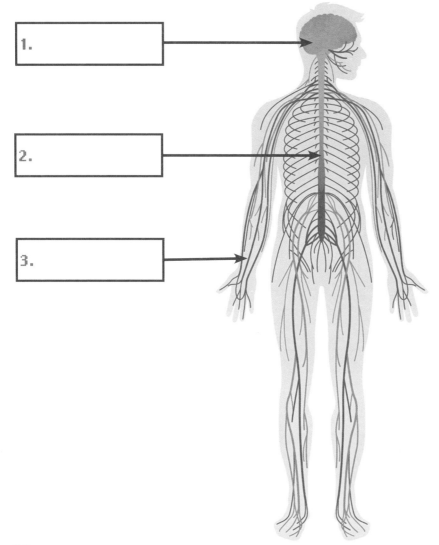

1.

2.

3.

SKELETAL SYSTEM

Read about the skeletal system. Circle the names of the bones in the puzzle.

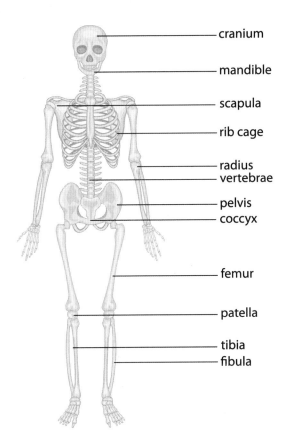

- cranium
- mandible
- scapula
- rib cage
- radius
- vertebrae
- pelvis
- coccyx
- femur
- patella
- tibia
- fibula

The skeletal system is made up of 106 bones. The bones give structure to the body. The bones protect the organs in the body.

```
V E R T E B R A E R D
P R L R X A P S N D T
D A W B I Y C N C N B
R J T B I A C R R Z J
I F I E P D A C T Y P
B T I U L N N S O E B
C Y L B I L U A L C R
A A Y U U I A V M U D
G L M Q D L I D M D Y
E W X A J S A E Z R B
B D R R G D F T P J D
```

cranium

mandible

scapula

rib cage

radius

vertebrae

pelvis

coccyx

femur

patella

tibia

fibula

MUSCULAR SYSTEM

Read about the muscular system. Answer the question with a full sentence.

Muscles help the body to walk, stand, and sit. There are hundreds of muscles in the body. Our muscles need movement and healthy foods to grow.

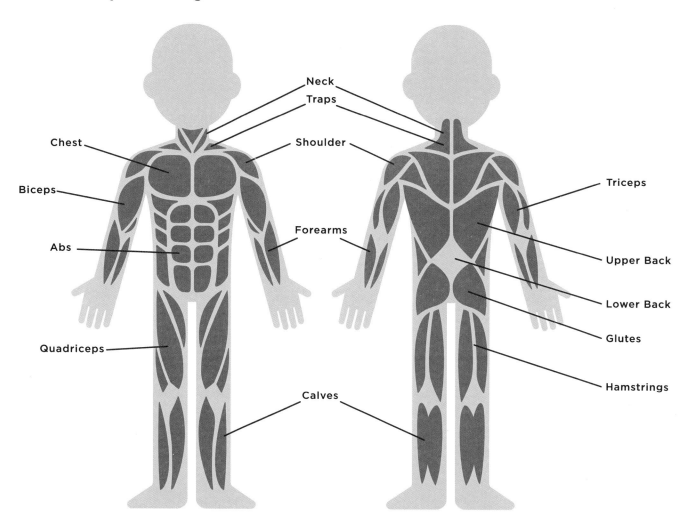

What is your favorite way to move your muscles?

_____

_____

_____

ECOSYSTEMS

Read about ecosystems. Draw arrows to show the transfer of energy through the ecosystem.

An ecosystem is an area where plants and animals interact with each other. Plants and animals also interact with the sun, soil, and water. In an ecosystem the sun provides energy to the plants. The plants use the energy from the sun to make their own food. Plants also get food from the soil. Some animals eat plants for energy. Other animals eat animals for energy. This transfer of energy in an ecosystem is called a food chain.

I like to eat cake!

PREDATORS AND PREY

Read about animal predators and their prey. Draw an arrow pointing from each predator to its prey. Hint: Some animals may have more than one prey.

All animals need food to live. Animals get their food from plants or other animals. A **predator** is an animal that hunts other animals to eat. A **prey** is an animal that is hunted as food. Some animals are both predators and prey for other animals. For example, when a hawk eats a snake, the hawk is a predator and the snake is the prey. But when an ocelot eats a hawk, the ocelot is the predator and the hawk is its prey.

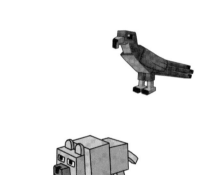

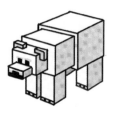

PREDATORS AND PREY

Read the sentences. Write which animal is the predator and which is the prey.

	Predator	Prey
1. An ocelot can be tamed with cod.		
2. The fish hid in the seaweed from the shark.		
3. The frog caught a fly with its long tongue.		
4. The bird watched over its eggs to keep the snake from eating them.		
5. The wolf stalked the rabbit.		
6. The worm inched across the grass before the bird ate it.		

ANIMAL ADAPTATIONS

Read about animal adaptations. Match each animal with its adaptation.

Animals have adaptations that help them survive in their environment. Adaptations can be physical features. Adaptations can be how an animal lives in its environment.

1.

2.

3.

4.

5.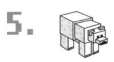

6.

A. sharp teeth for tearing flesh; thick fur to keep warm; hunt in packs

B. white fur to hide in the snow; sharp teeth for tearing flesh; thick fur to protect against cold

C. gills for breathing under water; fins for swimming

D. long eyelashes to keep sand out of eyes; humps for storing water

E. slithers to move across hot sand; sheds skin

F. sharp claws (talons) to hold prey in flight; sharp beak for tearing flesh

ANIMAL CAMOUFLAGE

Read about how animals use camouflage to protect themselves. Use the words in the word box to complete the sentences.

Some animals use camouflage to survive in the wild. Camouflage helps an animal blend into its environment. Sometimes camouflage helps the animal hide from its predators. Other times, camouflage helps an animal hide from its prey, so it can surprise it.

zebras	seahorse	owl
leopard	toad	praying mantis

1. The spotted coat of the _____ helps it to blend into its surroundings, so it can sneak up on its prey.

2. When _____ are in a herd, their stripes make them look like one large animal.

3. The _____ blends in with the leaf to keep from being seen.

4. The _____ blends into the trunk of the tree.

5. A _____ will flatten itself and blend in with fallen leaves and grass.

6. A _____ blends into the color of the coral floating in the ocean.

DENSITY AND BUOYANCY

Read about density and buoyancy. Write which items will float and which will sink.

Density describes how much space an object or substance takes up (its volume) in relation to the amount of matter in that object or substance (its mass). If you compare a solid block of iron ore to a large, empty cardboard box, the block would have more density. Objects with less density than water float in water. Objects with more density than water sink. Objects that float have buoyancy, which describes whether an object will float or not.

Things That Will Sink in Water

_____

_____

_____

Things That Will Float in Water

_____

_____

_____

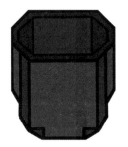

STATES OF MATTER

Study the diagram. Complete the paragraph about the states of matter, using words from the diagram.

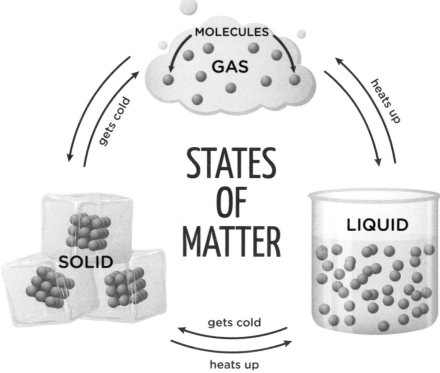

Matter is anything that has mass and takes up space.

Matter is made up of **(1)**_____. Matter can be

found in three states: solid, liquid, and gas. The molecules in a

(2)_____ have space between them and are always

moving. Gases have no shape. The air you breathe is made up of

gases. The molecules in **(3)**_____ move slower than

gases. They also have space between them. Liquid takes the shape of

its container. The molecules of a **(4)**_____ move very

slowly. A solid has shape. When a solid gets hot, it becomes a liquid.

When a liquid gets cold, it becomes a solid.

MIXTURES

Read about mixtures. Then study the Brewing Chart and list the ingredients needed for each of the potions.

A mixture is made by combining two or more ingredients. In the Minecraft world, potions are mixtures used to give the player extra skills or strengths.

Every potion needs:

_____   _____   _____   _____

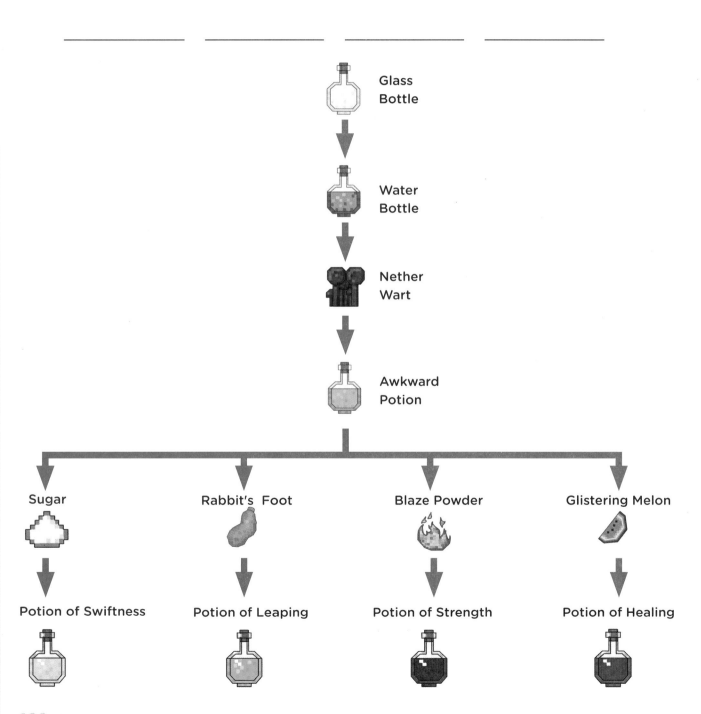

Glass Bottle

Water Bottle

Nether Wart

Awkward Potion

Sugar

Rabbit's Foot

Blaze Powder

Glistering Melon

Potion of Swiftness

Potion of Leaping

Potion of Strength

Potion of Healing

MIXTURES

Read the Brewing Chart on page 102. Answer the questions.

1. What potions' recipes are shown on the chart?

   _____ _____ _____ _____

2. What is the key ingredient to make the potion of Swiftness?

   _____

3. What is the key ingredient to make the potion of Leaping?

   _____

4. What is the key ingredient to make the potion of Strength?

   _____

5. What is the key ingredient to make the potion of Healing?

   _____

6. Which potion do you think is most useful? Tell why.

   _____

   _____

Perhaps I'll explore this outer world.

INSIDE THE EARTH

Read about the inside of the Earth. Label the layers of the Earth.

The inside of the Earth is made up of four different layers. The outer layer of the Earth is the **crust**. The crust is the thinnest layer. Our mountains and soil are part of the crust. Beneath the crust is the **mantle**. The mantle is the thickest layer. It is made up of molten rock. The center of the Earth is the core. It is split into the outer and inner core. The **outer core** is a liquid layer. The **inner core** is the hottest layer inside the Earth.

mantle	crust	inner core	outer core

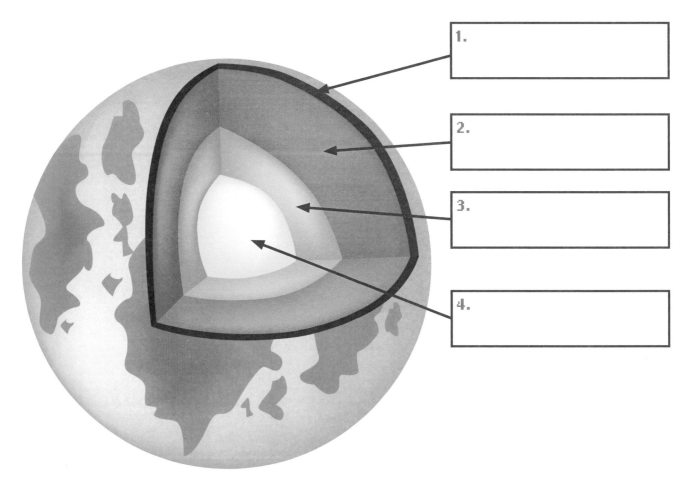

1.

2.

3.

4.

ROCKS

Read about rocks. Circle the rocks in the word puzzle.

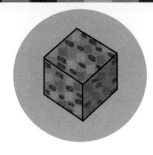

There are three types of rocks: igneous, sedimentary, and metamorphic. **Igneous** rocks are made when lava or magma cools. **Sedimentary** rocks are formed from sand, minerals, plants, and animals. They form into layers. Most rocks that you find are sedimentary. **Metamorphic** rocks are formed when igneous or sedimentary rocks undergo extreme heat or pressure.

igneous	sedimentary	metamorphic	
sandstone	obsidian	granite	basalt
	marble	magma	quartz

```
S G Z P T K Y N P L N B J
E B B D R B L N T D R G L
D C S A N D S T O N E G M
I I Y U P D J M A B R K D
M H L L O P E I B A D D T
E P R N M E D L N T W X X
N R B G Z I N I B T Y D G
T O M A S T T G Q R V Z J
A M L B S E K U I D A T A
R A O V J A A N Y Y N M D
Y T L D N R L J L G G T Y
D E W Y T N Q T N A T R W
Y M B Z J M L J M L Z M J
```

ROCKS

Read about each type of rock. Then check the boxes that describe each rock.

granite

hard

difficult to scratch

nonpermeable

can be shiny

clay

nonpermeable (or very low permeability)

soft

found in soil

dull

quartz

hard

shiny

nonpermeable

sandstone

can be soft or hard

dull

permeable

	granite	clay	quartz	sandstone
soft				
hard				
permeable (liquid **can** pass through)				
nonpermeable (liquid **cannot** pass through)				
shiny				
dull				

FOSSILS

Read about fossils. Draw a line to match each animal to its fossil.

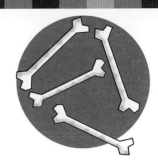

Fossils are the remains of plants and animals. Fossils are found deep in the layers of sedimentary rock.

1.

2.

3.

4.

A.

B.

C.

D.

VOLCANOES

Read about volcanoes. Circle the related words in the puzzle.

A volcano is an opening in earth's surface from which **gas**, **lava**, and **magma** can flow. Most volcanoes are found in mountains. Volcanoes can be different shapes and sizes. Some volcanoes form on flat land. Most form on fault lines or cracks in the earth. There are even some volcanoes in the ocean. The three major types of volcanoes are **composite**, **shield**, and **dome**.

volcano	lava	fault	shield
gas	magma	composite	dome

```
C O M P O S I T E
V S A G B R M Z J
M O P T L B D Y T
Y L L D L P W D T
L M M C D U L Y G
J L A O A E A L R
Y P M G I N A F Y
L E T H M V O M T
R T S L A A B P L
```

EARTHQUAKES

Read about earthquakes. Then label the diagram.

Pistons move blocks in the Minecraft world.

If you have ever felt the ground move, you have felt an earthquake. Earth's crust is made up of tectonic plates. These plates are always moving. All around the plates are **faults** or cracks in Earth's surface. Most earthquakes happen on the faults. The **focus** is where an earthquake begins deep inside the Earth. The **epicenter** is where the earthquake happens on the surface of the Earth. An earthquake sends **seismic waves** out beyond the epicenter. Seismic waves move the ground many miles from the epicenter.

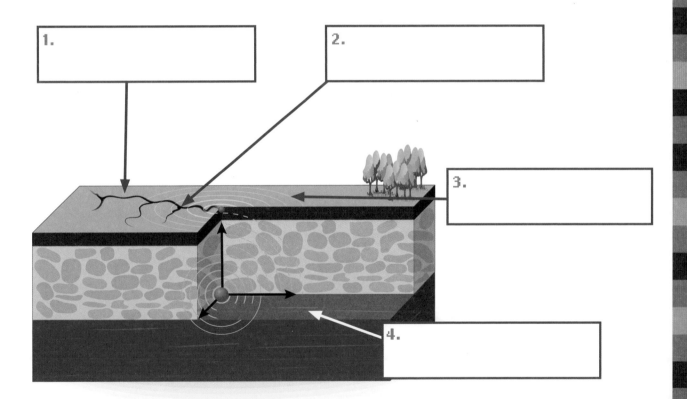

1.

2.

3.

4.

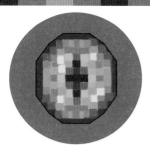

HURRICANES

Read about hurricanes. Draw a hurricane. Label the eye. Draw arrows showing the direction of the winds.

Hurricanes are large storms that form over the ocean. They are made up of strong winds. The center of a hurricane is known as the **eye**. This is also the calmest part of the storm. The winds of a hurricane blow counterclockwise around the eye.

TORNADOES

Read about tornadoes. Then review the statements. Write T if the statement is true and F if the statement is false.

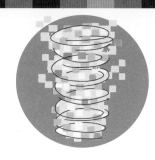

Tornadoes are dangerous and powerful wind storms. The wind of a tornado forms in the clouds during a thunderstorm. As it spins, it forms a funnel shape. A tornado extends from a cloud to the ground.

1. Tornadoes start on the ground. _____

2. Tornadoes are spinning winds. _____

3. Thunderstorm is another name for a tornado. _____

4. Tornadoes start on the ocean. _____

5. Tornadoes are funnel-shaped. _____

6. Tornadoes are good for flying kites. _____

JUST FOR FUN

Q: How are the creepers like tornadoes?

A: They are sometimes called twisters.

TSUNAMIS

Read about tsunamis. Number the steps that tell how a tsunami happens.

A **tsunami** is a series of waves. These waves are most often caused by earthquakes below the ocean. The ground on one side of a fault line suddenly rises or falls. All of the water above it does the same, creating giant waves. The waves can be so large that they destroy homes and buildings along the coast.

_____ Large waves form.

_____ First an earthquake occurs below the ocean.

_____ Large waves hit the shore.

_____ A section of the ocean floor rises or falls.

_____ The ocean water rises or falls.

WEATHER WORDS

Complete the word search puzzle.

blizzard	thunderstorm	drizzle	rain	hurricane
flood	sleet	hail	snow	tornado	wind

```
T T Q N T T L S Y N P D B
H B Y W P D L K F W R Q T
U X Y K I E J L Y A R D X
N D Y T E N O X Z M L B H
D N R T O O D Z W I Z U M
E I Y I D D I K A O R J R
R A T L Z L A H J R N R T
S R R J B Z N N I D B S M
T Q T J V Q L C R D X Q T
O Z X R T Y A E B O D Z Q
R D M Z Z N B M Q N T J D
M P L Y E D G J B R Z R R
```

MAGNETS

Read about magnets. Draw a line from the magnet to the objects it will attract.

A magnet is an object that produces a magnetic field and pulls, or attracts, another object toward it. Magnets attract certain strong metals, including iron, nickel, cobalt, and some steel. Weaker metals such as aluminum, brass, copper, gold, lead, and silver are not magnetic.

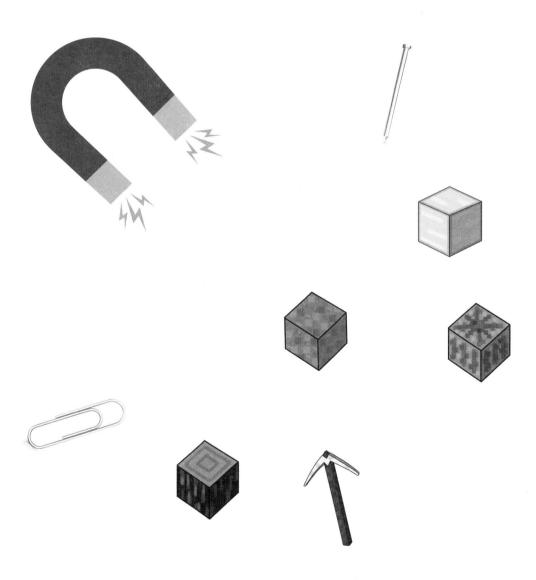

MAGNETISM

Read about magnets. Circle if the magnets will attract or repel.

Every magnet has a north and a south pole. Opposite poles attract. Like poles repel.

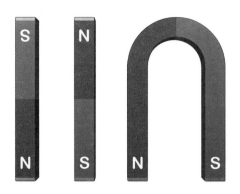

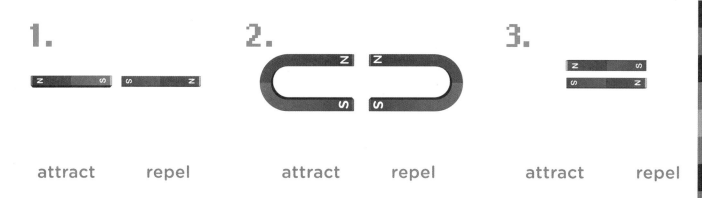

1.

attract   repel

2.

attract   repel

3.

attract   repel

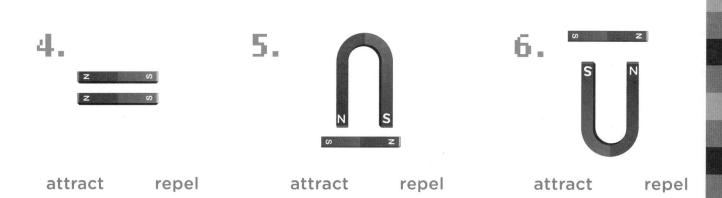

4.

attract   repel

5.

attract   repel

6.

attract   repel

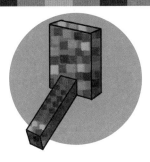

ENERGY

Read about energy. Then write about how things in the Minecraft world get and use energy.

Energy is the ability to do work. All things need energy to move. People, animals, and plants need energy to grow and move. Machines need energy to move. Cars need energy to move. Ovens use energy to cook food. There are many types of energy. Energy is divided into two groups: renewable energy and nonrenewable energy.

Renewable Energy Sources	Nonrenewable Energy Sources
solar energy (from the sun)	oil (petroleum)
geothermal energy (from heat inside the earth)	natural gas
wind energy	coal
biomass (from plants)	nuclear energy
hydropower (from moving water)	

_____

_____

_____

_____

_____

ENERGY

Read about energy. Draw a picture to show different ways that you give and use energy.

People use energy for many things. People need energy to live. We use energy to keep warm, to eat, and to have fun.

How do you use energy to keep warm?	How do you use energy to keep or prepare food?
How do you use food as energy?	How do you use energy to have fun?

ELECTRICAL CIRCUITS

Read about electrical circuits. Label the parts of a circuit.

A circuit is a path that allows electricity to flow. All circuits include a **source** of electricity, such as a battery, connected at both the positive and negative ends. Circuits also need wires or other materials that allow electricity to travel through. These are called **conductors**. If any one of these parts is missing or not connected, the electricity will not flow. When the circuit is complete, or closed, the **device** (such as the lightbulb below) can use the electricity to do work. Some circuits also have a **switch** that turn the electricity on or off by opening or closing the circuit.

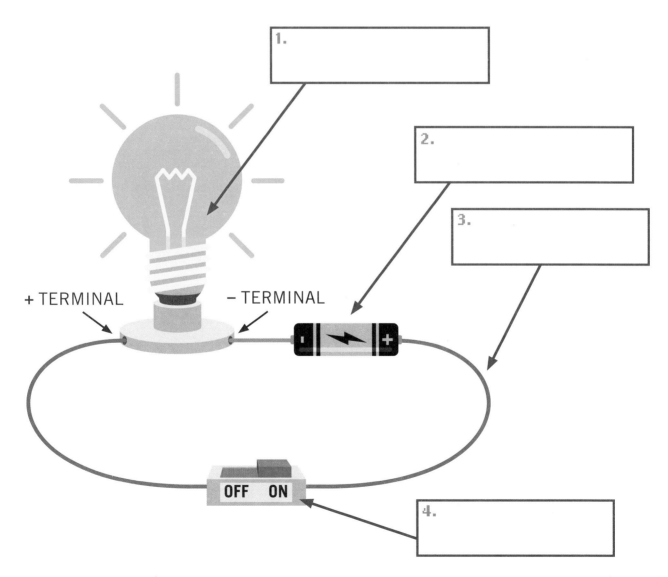

1.

2.

3.

4.

+ TERMINAL

− TERMINAL

OFF   ON

ELECTRICAL CIRCUITS

Explain why the circuit will or will not light the bulb.

1.

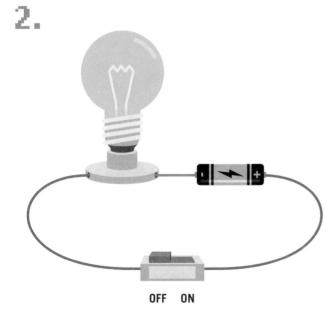

OFF   ON

_____

_____

_____

_____

_____

2.

OFF   ON

_____

_____

_____

_____

Watch me teleport!

ALEXANDER BELL

Read about Alexander Bell. Study the meaning of the word parts in the chart. Draw a line to match the words to their meanings.

Alexander Bell loved to study sound. His interest in sound began when he was young. Because of his interest in sound, he invented the first telephone. He also invented a metal detector, audiometer, and a tool to find icebergs. In addition, he experimented with aeronautics and hydrofoils.

tele – at a distance	detect – uncover	aero – air	hydro – water
phone – sound	audio – hearing	naut – traveler	meter – measure

1. telephone

2. detector

3. audiometer

4. aeronautics

5. hydrofoil

A. a tool to measure hearing

B. a tool that uncovers something

C. a water boat with wings

D. the study of air travel

E. a tool for transmitting sound at a distance

THOMAS EDISON

Read about Thomas Edison. Then think of a problem you have and design a way to make it better.

I invented this minecart!

Thomas Edison was a great inventor. He made 1,093 inventions. He invented a lightbulb, a phonograph, and a motion picture camera. Many inventors improved on his inventions. Because of his inventions, we have lights in our homes, music players, and movies. All inventors start with a problem to solve. Inventors figure out a way to do something better.

MY PROBLEM

WHAT MY INVENTION DOES

MY INVENTION

HOW MY INVENTION WORKS

SKETCH OF MY INVENTION

I love my crafting table!

JOSEPHINE COCHRANE

Read about Josephine Cochrane. Then write about an invention you couldn't live without.

Josephine Cochrane loved to have dinner parties, but she didn't love doing dishes. One night after a dinner party, she had a huge stack of dishes that needed to be washed. At the time, each dish had to be washed, rinsed, and dried one at a time. "There must be another way," Josephine thought. This thought led her to invent the first dishwasher.

I can't imagine living without a _____ .
name the invention

This invention _____ .
tell what the invention does

It makes my life easier by _____ .
tell how the invention makes your life easier

It also _____ .
tell something else about the invention

This invention is the best because _____ .
sum up what's great
about the invention

WRIGHT BROTHERS

Read about the Wright brothers. Then write and draw about what you dream of doing one day.

Orville and Wilbur Wright grew up inventing things. They also liked to watch birds fly. They dreamed of flying one day too. And they did. The Wright brothers invented the first flying machine that could carry a human. But this wasn't an easy task. It took many years and many failures to finally invent a successful flying machine. This invention led to many other inventions, including the airplanes we fly in today.

I dream of _____ .

I see myself _____ .

To make the dream come true, I _____

_____ .

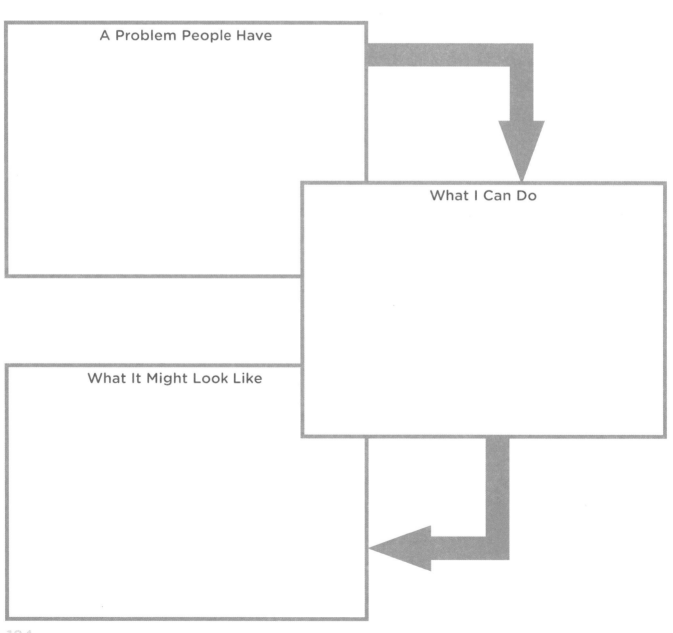

I will fight to defend others!

BESSIE GRIFFIN

Read about Bessie Griffin. Then write and draw about how you would like to help others.

Bessie Griffin wanted to help people. She became a physical therapist to help people with injuries. She worked with many soldiers who were injured in World War II. Some of the soldiers had lost arms or hands in the war. Bessie taught the soldiers how to use their feet to do things. She also invented a device to help people without hands feed themselves. Bessie invented other things to help people.

A Problem People Have

What I Can Do

What It Might Look Like

INVENTORS' TIMELINE

Read about the inventors. Then place their names on the timeline.

[Empty box]

[Empty box]

1870 ———————————————————————————— **1970**

1880 | 1890 | 1900 | 1910 | 1920 | 1930 | 1940 | 1950 | 1960

[Empty box]

[Empty box]

1. In 1876, Alexander Bell spoke on a telephone he invented.

2. In 1880, Thomas Edison invented a light bulb.

3. In 1886, Josephine Cochrane invented the dishwasher.

4. In 1903, the Wright brothers made their first successful flight.

5. In 1951, Bessie Griffin invented a feeding device that helped people without hands feed themselves.

You can read more about these inventors on pages 120–124 or on the Internet.

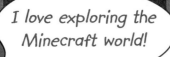

I love exploring the Minecraft world!

EXPLORERS

Read about the early explorers. Circle the names of the explorers in the word puzzle.

Between 1500 and 1600, many countries in Europe sent explorers to discover new lands. These explorers sailed ships across the oceans. They wanted to find trading partners. They were looking for gold and treasures. They were hoping to claim new land. The box below lists some of the most famous explorers.

Christopher Columbus	Sir Francis Drake	Hernan Cortes
Vasco da Gama	Ferdinand Magellan	Marco Polo
Juan Ponce de Leon	Francisco Pizarro	Vasco Nunez de Balbo

```
S V A S C O N U N E Z D E B A L B O A
Q U B O S E T R O C N A N R E H F Z J
E K B R R K J T L Z K N T T M E J N N
Q K X M B R R B P L P Q N V R T Y Z L
V Q A Q U K A P T X Y T T D Z J G B J
Y A B R M L G Z M R T J I V U Y B N B
X Y S Z D J O Y I D L N R A Z R L Y M
R K M C R S W C B P A M N M D X J V Z
Y L D X O N I W R N O P L Z J L Y Q D
N D L L T D R C D E O C Z N M B T J K
D Y L Q D B A M N N H S Z Z N G O G
D Y L L B R A G C A Y P W I J J L V V
K W L J N G J E A J R M O B C O M N D
R M D Y E Q D B T M Y F P T P N D Y J
Z T L L V E X W T B A Z R O S L A Y P
R G L B L M Y X T B K W C I D I K R L
J A Y E J Y Y B P Q M R T X S X R G F
N R O M M Y Q M Y R A L N R X K V H N
V N B Q L Q N D R M T Y L T X N B P C
```

JAMESTOWN

Read about Jamestown. Answer the questions.

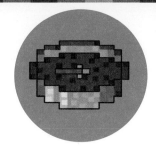

      Hundreds of years ago, many Europeans risked their lives to cross the Atlantic Ocean. Some of them wanted to build homes and businesses in the North American colonies. They hoped to improve their lives. In December 1606, three ships left England. There were 104 men on the ships. The ships landed on the shores of Virginia in April 1607. The first English colony was settled in Jamestown, Virginia. About 14,000 Powhatan Indians lived in this area.

1. Three ships sailed from England to Virginia with a total of 104 men. If the number of men on each ship was about equal, how many men may have been on each ship? _____

2. About how long did it take to sail from England to Virginia? _____

_____

3. The journey across the Atlantic Ocean was about 6,000 miles. If the ships traveled the same distance each day (144 days), how many miles would they have traveled each day? _____

4. About how many more Indians than Englishmen lived in Virginia in 1607?

_____

COLONIAL LIFE

Colonial life was different than life today. Draw a line from what we have today to what was used in colonial times for the same purpose.

1. 🛋️

2. 🚗

3. 📝

4. 💿

5. ✈️

A.

B.

C.

D.

E.

THIRTEEN COLONIES

Unscramble the names of the thirteen colonies to label them on the map.

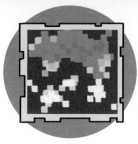

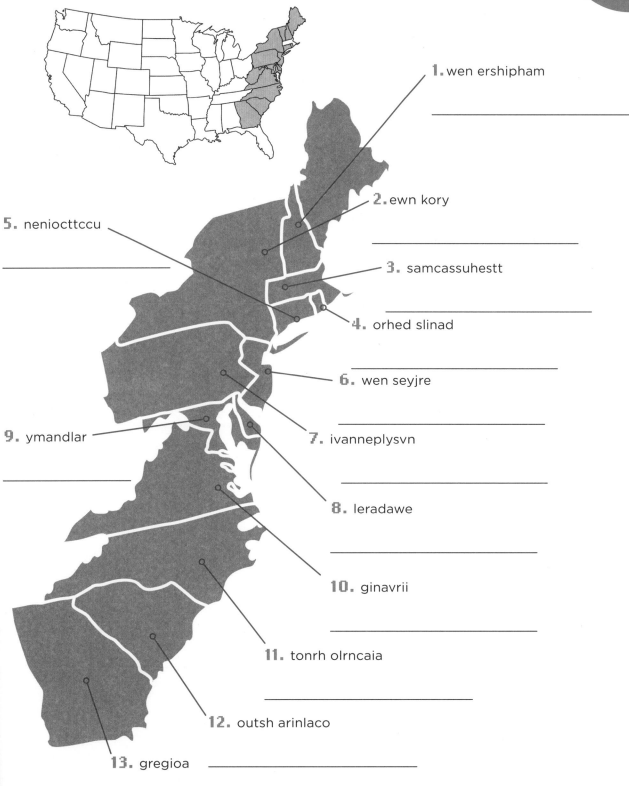

1. wen ershipham

_____

2. ewn kory

_____

3. samcassuhestt

_____

4. orhed slinad

_____

5. neniocttccu

_____

6. wen seyjre

_____

7. ivanneplysvn

_____

8. leradawe

_____

9. ymandlar

_____

10. ginavrii

_____

11. tonrh olrncaia

_____

12. outsh arinlaco

_____

13. gregioa _____

_____

AMERICAN REVOLUTION

Read about the causes of the American Revolution. Draw a line to match the dates to events that led to the American Revolution.

By 1700, life in the thirteen colonies was very busy. All of the colonists paid taxes to the British Government. But by 1765, many of the colonists started to think that the King of England was taxing them too much. They thought it was unfair that they had to pay taxes but did not get any say in the decisions of the government.

1. 1765
Stamp Act

2. 1770
Boston Massacre

3. 1773
Boston Tea Party

4. 1776
Declaration of Independence

A. To protest the taxing of tea, several colonists dumped a load of tea into the Boston Harbor.

B. Because of the taxes, tensions were high between the colonists and the British soldiers. During this conflict, British soldiers killed five colonists in Boston.

C. Thomas Jefferson and other leaders of the colonies declared the colonies' independence from Britain.

D. This act said that every paper needed to have the British seal or stamp on it. It was the first tax put on the colonists. It taxed all newspapers and paper documents.

AMERICAN REVOLUTION

Read to learn about some of the key people in the American Revolution. Then use the information to solve the crossword puzzle.

John Adams
Leader of American Independence; 2nd U.S. President

Benjamin Franklin
Founder; Statesman and an inventor

Patrick Henry
Founder; Colonel during the war; Lawyer

Thomas Jefferson
Author of the Declaration of Independence; 3rd U.S. President

Paul Revere
Member of Sons of Liberty; Announced the British were coming

George Washington
General in the war; 1st U.S. President

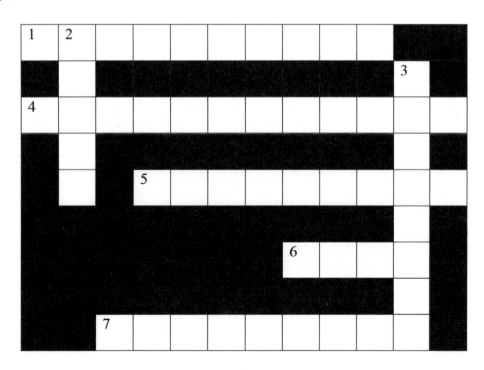

ACROSS

1 First U.S. President
4 Colonel in the war
5 Leader of the U.S.
6 First name of man who warned about the British
7 Wrote the Declaration of Independence

DOWN

2 Second U.S. President
3 A statesman and inventor

LOUISIANA PURCHASE

Read about the Louisiana Purchase. Then follow the directions.

In 1803, Thomas Jefferson was the third president of the United States. The U.S. was made up of 17 states. Jefferson wanted the U.S. to grow. He purchased a large piece of land from France. This land was called the Louisiana Territory. The Louisiana Purchase almost doubled the size of the U.S.

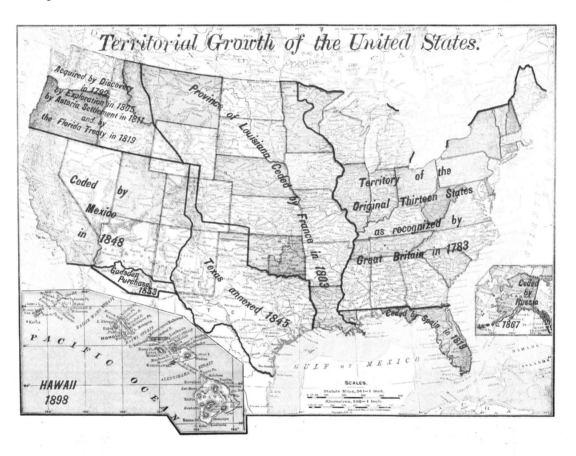

1. Draw a star on the map where your state is located.

2. Was your state part of the Louisiana purchase? Explain.

_____

_____

_____

_____

TRAIL OF TEARS

Read about the Trail of Tears. Complete the word puzzle with the names of the tribes that were forced to give up their land.

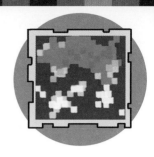

The Trail of Tears describes a time in the history of the United States. To help America grow, President Andrew Jackson made up a law. It was called the Indian Removal Policy. This law forced many Native American tribes to give up their land and to move to land that is now Oklahoma. The tribes included the Chickasaw, Seminole, Creek, Choctaw, and Cherokee. Many people lost not only their land, but their lives.

T
E
A
R
S

LEWIS AND CLARK

Read about the Lewis and Clark Expedition. Write what you think one of their journal entries along the way might have said.

After the purchase of the Louisiana Territory, President Jefferson wanted to learn more about the land to the West. He asked Meriwether Lewis and William Clark to find a route to the Pacific Ocean. **(1)** They started in St. Louis. **(2)** They traveled west on the Missouri River. Because the river flowed east, it was difficult. Then they came to the end of the river. **(3)** They came to the Rocky Mountains. Travel was hard through the Rocky Mountains. **(4)** They continued on foot until they reached the Columbia River. **(5)** Finally, they reached the Pacific Ocean. Lewis and Clark and the other men on their expedition learned a lot about the land and the Native Americans. They created maps and kept journals.

_____

_____

_____

_____

_____

_____

_____

_____

THE LONE STAR STATE

Read about Texas. Color the state. Add pictures of things you think of when you think of Texas.

Texas was once part of Mexico. In 1835, American Samuel Austin started a colony in Texas. There was a lot of fighting between the Americans who moved to Texas and the Mexicans. At the Battle of the Alamo, 180 Texans held off 4,000 Mexicans for thirteen days, before being killed. Still, Texas declared its independence from Mexico in 1836. Many battles continued. Sam Houston convinced the other Texan leaders to join the United States. In 1845, Texas became the 28th state. It is the second largest state.

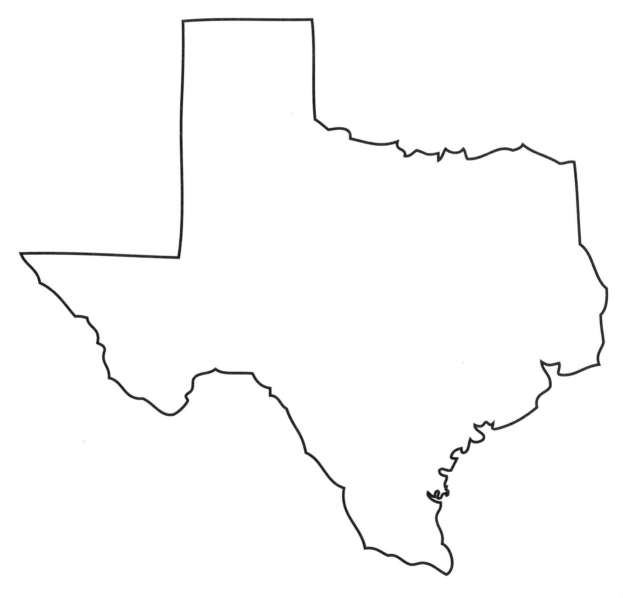

OREGON TRAIL

Read about the Oregon Trail. Then compare how starting a new life out West like the settlers did is like exploring in the Minecraft world.

The Oregon Trail was actually a group of trails used by the Native Americans, fur traders, and settlers looking to own land in the West. Many of the Native Americans and fur traders traveled on foot or by horseback. Settlers packed all their belongs in covered wagons. The journey was long and hard. It could take up to six months. There were many dangers along the way. Some of the dangers included sickness, drowning, weather, snakebites, and injuries. There is a computer game called The Oregon Trail. In this game, the player becomes the Wagon Master. The object is to survive the dangers of traveling along the Oregon Trail in the 1800s.

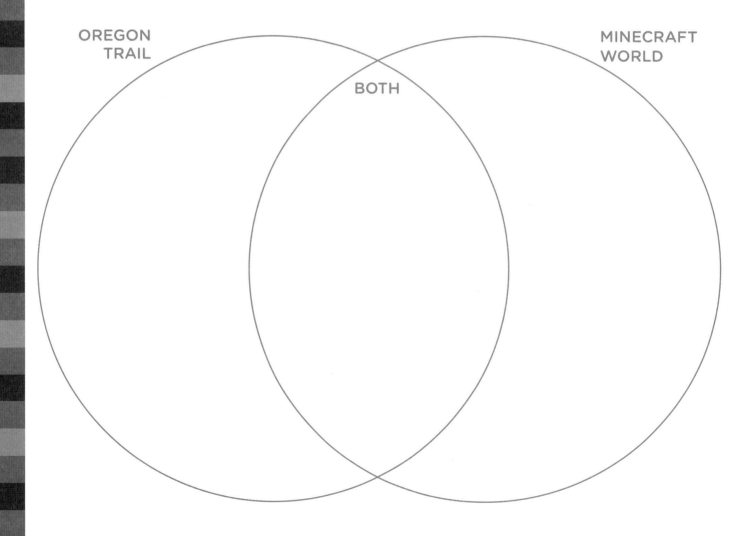

OREGON TRAIL

BOTH

MINECRAFT WORLD

GOLD RUSH

Read about the California Gold Rush. Write the directions for crafting a gold suit.

   In 1848, gold was discovered at Sutter's Mill in California. Because of this discovery, about 80,000 people traveled west. They hoped to find fields of gold. Miners used picks, shovels, and pans to find gold. Many people moved to the land, and California became the 31st state. Soon many schools, churches, businesses, and roads were built.

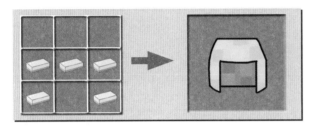

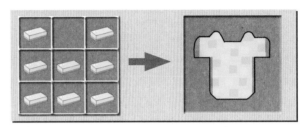

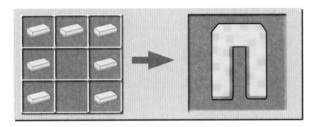

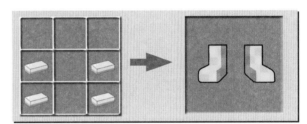

_____

_____

_____

_____

_____

_____

_____

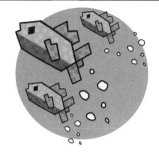

ALASKA

Read about Alaska. Then answer the questions.

In 1959, Alaska became the 49th state of the United States. It is the largest state. Texas is the next largest state. Texas is half the size of Alaska.

1. What country does Alaska connect to? _____

2. What two oceans surround Alaska? _____ _____

3. What seas surround Alaska? _____ _____

   _____

4. Find your state. About how many of your states will fit in Alaska?

   _____

HAWAII

Read about Hawaii. Unscramble the islands' names and label the map.

In 1959, Hawaii became the 50th state of the United States. It is located in the Pacific Ocean. Hawaii is the world's largest island chain. It is made up of 132 islands. But only seven of the islands have people living on them. The islands are Hawaii, Maui, Molokai, Lanai, Oahu, Kauai, and Niihau.

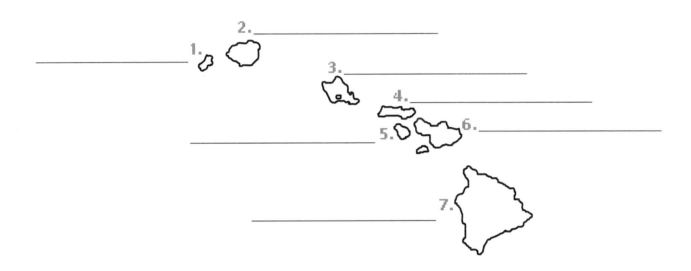

2. _____

1. _____

3. _____

4. _____

5. _____   6. _____

7. _____

1. ihinau	**5.** aanil
2. aaiuak	**6.** umai
3. hauo	**7.** iiwaha
4. akioolam	

MY STATE REPORT

Research information about your state. Complete the graphic organizer by writing or drawing the answers.

MY STATE

WHAT IT LOOKS LIKE

ITS LOCATION

JUST THE FACTS

Governor:_____

Capital:_____

Date of Statehood:_____

Population:_____

Size (Area): _____

Slogan: _____

Large Cities:

_____

_____

_____

Interesting Fact:

_____

_____

STATE FLAG

STATE FLOWER

STATE BIRD

VISIT MY STATE

Create a poster advertising your state. Be sure to point out key points of interest and reasons to visit.

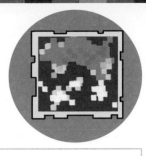

Maps are a bird's eye view of a place.

CREATING A MAP

Draw a map of the desert temple area shown.

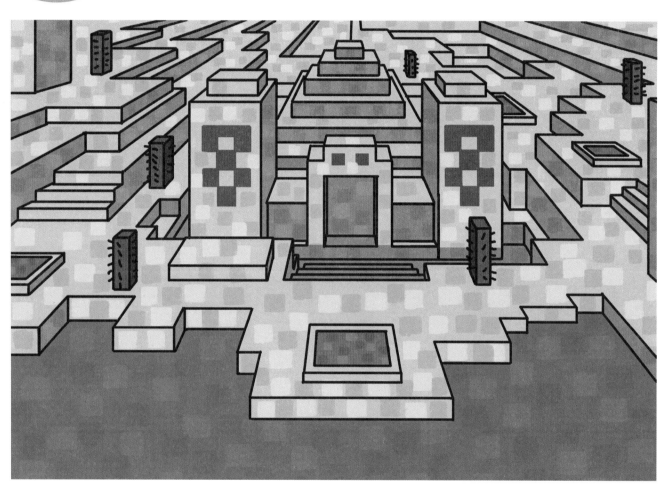

READING A GRID MAP

Read this map of a Minecraft world. Answer the questions.

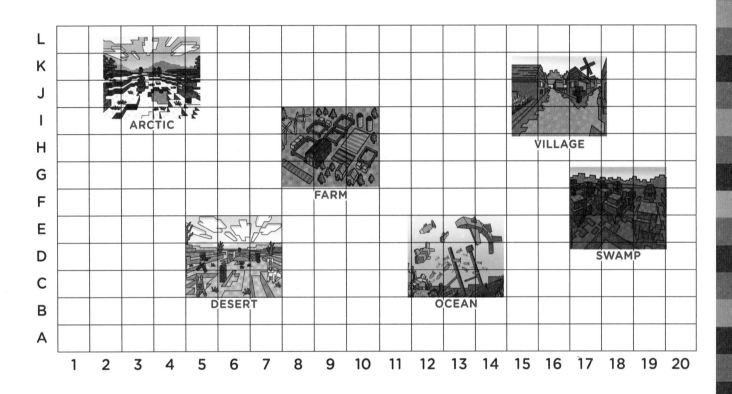

1. Where are you if you are at 13C? _____

2. Where are you if you are at 4K? _____

3. Where are you if you are at 18F? _____

4. Where are you if you are at 15J? _____

5. Where are you if you are at 6D? _____

6. Where are you if you are at 9H? _____

LATITUDE AND LONGITUDE

Read this map. Fill in the red boxes to complete the degrees of latitude and longitude lines.

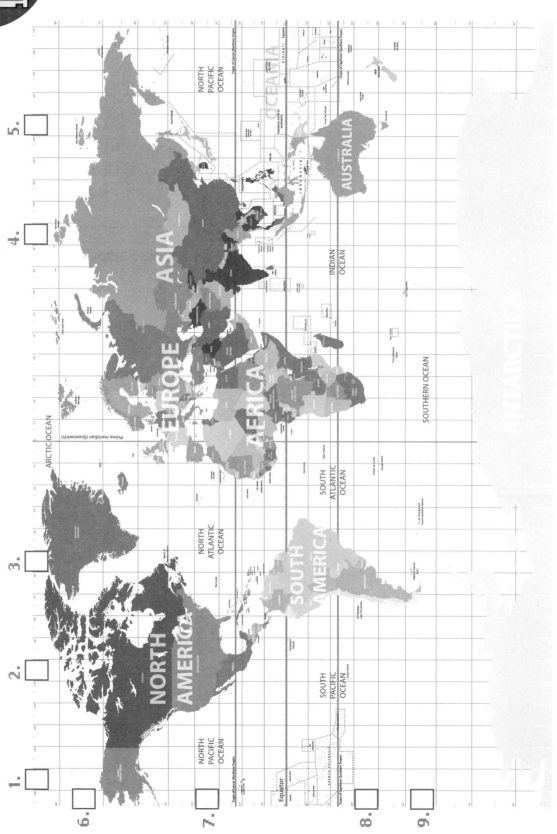

LATITUDE AND LONGITUDE

Read about longitude and latitude lines. Use the map on page 144 to answer the questions.

Latitude and longitude are imaginary lines that circle the Earth. They are used to find location. Longitude lines run north and south. Latitude lines run east and west. These lines are measured in degrees. The **equator** is at 0° latitude. The **prime meridian** is at 0° longitude.

1. What imaginary lines run north and south on a map? _____

2. What imaginary lines run east and west on a map? _____

3. What is the name of 0° latitude? _____

4. What is the name of 0° longitude? _____

5. What country is at 30°N and 100°W? _____

6. What continent is at 30°S and 100°E? _____

7. What continent is at 10°S and 30°E? _____

8. What continent is at 30°N and 100°E? _____

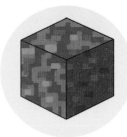

GLOBES AND MAPS

Compare a globe and a map. Write the words and statements in the correct space in the Venn diagram. Remember, write a statement that is true about both in the intersecting space.

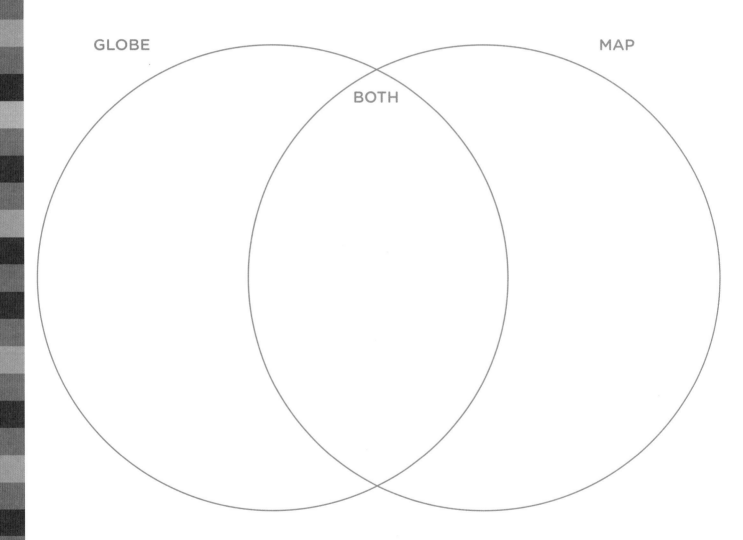

GLOBE

BOTH

MAP

WANTS AND NEEDS

Read about wants and needs. Write five things you have that are needs and five things you have that are wants.

Needs are things that are necessary to live. We need food, water, air, and shelter. Some people need medicines or medical equipment to live. Wants are things that make life more comfortable, more fun, and more interesting. But we do not need wants to live. Sometimes wants and needs are confusing. We need food to live and candy is food. But we don't need to have candy to live. Healthy foods are a need. Candy and other treats are a want. We need clothes to live. But we don't need expensive clothes. Families decide how to pay for needs and some wants.

WANTS	NEEDS

BUYING WANTS AND NEEDS

You have $100 to spend. Write a list to show how you will spend your money.

1.

$25.00
Groceries for a week

2.

$10.00
Bicycle

3.

$25.00
Rent for a week

4.

$1.00
Apple

5.

$10.00
Clothing

6.

$25.00
Water and electricity

7.

$5.00
Compass

8.

$10.00
Dinner at a restaurant

9.

$1.00
Cookie

10.

$2.00
Fun and games

11.

$5.00
Saving for a vacation

12.

$5.00
Saving for emeralds

MY SHOPPING LIST

_____

_____

_____

_____

_____

_____

_____

_____

_____

_____

GOODS AND SERVICES

Look at what Steve purchased. Circle whether each purchase was a good or service.

A **good** is something that is made or grown.

A **service** is work that is done for others.

1. watering can   good   service

2. protection in the village   good   service

3. care for his farm animals   good   service

4. help transporting gems from the mine   good   service

5. pickaxe   good   service

6. potion   good   service

7. map   good   service

8. instruction on finding the cave   good   service

ANSWER KEY

PAGE 5

1. Nitwit is a villager with no profession. 2. Fishing rods are tools used to catch fish. 3. The job of the Ender crystal is to heal the Ender Dragon. 4. The player built a lava pit and the zombie fell into it.

PAGE 6

1. D; 2. F; 3. A; 4. C; 5. E; 6. B

PAGE 7

1. bee/tree; 2. Ten/pen; 3. cow/plow; 4. rabbit/habit; 5. gears/shears; 6. witch/ditch

PAGE 8

1. unseen; 2. review; 3. preschool; 4. impossible; 5. misbehave; 6. disagree

PAGE 9

1. review; 2. underwater; 3. misspell; 4. preheat; 5. unhappy; 6. disagree

PAGE 10

1. excitement/retirement/agreement; 2. windy/dirty/noisy; 3. childish; 4. kindness/likeness; 5. friendly/kindly/likely 6. friendship

PAGE 11

1. hugging; 2. jumped; 3. slipped; 4. sliding; 5. hopping; 6. digging; 7. beautiful; 8. smiled; 9. caring; 10. cutting

PAGE 12

1. unforgettable, E; 2. indescribable, A; 3. misspelling, F; 4. unfriendly, B; 5. unhelpful, C; 6. uncontrollable, D

PAGE 13

1. black/smith; 2. danc/ing; 3. zom/bie; 4.vil/lag/er; 5. but/ter/fly; 6. cob/web; 7. em/er/alds; 8. En/der/man

PAGE 14

1. B; 2. A; 3. A; 4. A; 5. B

PAGE 15

1. B; 2. A; 3. A; 4. B; 5. A

PAGE 16

1. apple/bread/butterfly/carrot; 2. clock/emerald/flower/goat; 3. iron/lava/lever/magma; 4. moon/ocelot/orb/potato

PAGE 17

1. B; 2. B; 3. B; 4. A; 5. A; 6. A

PAGE 18

1. ate/eight; 2. meet/meat; 3. knew/new; 4. know/no; 5. their/there/they're; 6. two/too/to

PAGE 19

```
K N I G H T Z Y E R S N R W
N E T H G I E W C L O E D T
J B U Y J D R W A L O A A D
N G R L I Y D H E Y D H D Q
K T B A B R N P P R T V R
M A T K K Z T L P E H E E S
D J E W Y E X E C G B W R J
R R N R X R L E I W E O Z T
W A I T B L I N O L D Q J T
D E J R T P T U B E Y L T N
O J L V D V L V Z Q M R T L
O K R A K D D B D R B X V D
W Q V J T J L T N G Y K B N
```

PAGE 20

Steve, farm, animals, cows, sheep, wheat, pigs, carrots, beetroots, chickens, seeds, animals, baby, babies, minutes, Steve, pens, animals, barn, coop

PAGE 21

1. hissed; 2. attack; 3. explodes; 4. climb; 5. runs; 6. flashes

PAGE 22

Answers may vary. Possible answers include:
1. yellow, spotted; 2. five, white; 3. long, green;
4. old, creepy; 5. cute, pink

PAGE 23

1. Creeper <u>hissed</u> <u>loudly</u>. 2. Iron golem <u>awkwardly</u> <u>handed</u> the flower to the villager. 3. Alex <u>gently</u> <u>cared</u> for the animals. 4. The baby zombie villagers <u>played</u> <u>happily</u>. 5. Alex <u>carefully</u> <u>put</u> the diamond armor in the chest. 6. The bee <u>buzzed</u> <u>quickly</u> from flower to flower.

PAGE 24

1. and; 2. but; 3. or; 4. and; 5. so; 6. but

PAGE 25

1. in; 2. behind; 3. on; 4. under; 5. around; 6. over

PAGE 26

1. Steve collected wood (from) the forest to build a shelter. 2. Steve climbed (up) a tree to get away (from) the mobs. 3. You can find a witch hut (in) the Swampland Biome. 4. (Inside) the witch hut, you can find a crafting table. 5. Horses can be found (in) the Plains Biome. 6. If you click (on) a horse, you can ride it.

PAGE 27

1. <u>The Minecraft world</u> <u>has many mobs</u>. 2. <u>You can tame some mobs</u>. 3. <u>Some mobs</u> <u>can be eaten</u>. 4. <u>Creeper</u> <u>likes to screech and explode</u>. 5. <u>Utility mobs</u> <u>can help a player</u>. 6. <u>Iron Golem</u> <u>is a utility mob</u>.

PAGE 28

1. S; 2. F; 3. S; 4. S; 5. F; 6. F

PAGE 29

1. Steve found a diamond, so he put it in his cart. 2. Steve wanted to tame a creeper, but it exploded. 3. Steve can go to the Desert Biome, or he can go to the Jungle Biome. 4. Steve likes to play in the village, but Alex likes to play on the farm.

PAGE 30

1. Zombies are undead hostile mobs. 2. Watch out for baby zombies! 3. Baby zombies are even more dangerous than big zombies. 4. On Halloween, zombies put pumpkins on their heads.

PAGE 31

Cave spiders live ^(in) abandoned mineshafts. they climb walls and (hid) [sp hide] in cobwebs. (The) [sp they] (all so) [sp also] swim (so) very fast. They spawn (frum) [sp from] monster spawners. They (attak) [sp attack] by jumping at (there) [sp their] target. They are very poisonous. When killed, they can drop string or ^(a) spider ^('s) eye.

PAGE 32

1. bird; 2. bat; 3. dog; 4. horse; 5. mule; 6. bunny; 7. cat; 8. fox

PAGE 33

1. C; 2. E; 3. A; 4. B; 5. D

PAGE 34

1. B; 2. A; 3. B; 4. A; 5. B; 6. B

PAGE 35

1. A; 2. A; 3. B; 4. B; 5. A; 6. B

PAGES 36-41

Answers will vary.

151

PAGE 42

1. Get a crafting table, five glass blocks, three obsidian blocks, and a nether star. 2. Place the three obsidian blocks along the bottom row of the crafting table. 3. Place the nether star in the center of the table. 4. Place the rest of the glass blocks on the table. 5. Set the beacon on a pyramid to activate it.

PAGE 43

PAGE 44

1. D; 2. C; 3. E; 4. A; 5. B

PAGE 45

1. you need put it in an oven.
2. If you want to trade with a villager,
3. they only will attack if attacked.
4. If you want to tame a horse,
5. you can make rabbit stew.
6. When attacked,

PAGE 46

Answers will vary.

PAGE 47

1. 60; 2. 70; 3. 30; 4. 20; 5. 90; 6. 20; 7. 80; 8. 20; 9. 100; 10. 10; 11. 70; 12. 50; 13. 70; 14. 30; 15. 40; 16. 40; 17. 10; 18. 70

PAGE 48

1. 6,000 + 700 + 20 + 5; 2. 1,000 + 400 + 80 + 9; 3. 8,000 + 40 + 6; 4. 9,000 + 900 + 90 + 9; 5. 4,000 + 300 + 90 + 1; 6. 2,000 + 800 + 10 + 4; 7. 3,000 + 700 + 20 + 9; 8. 5,000 + 600 +2; 9. 7,000 + 900 + 40 + 7

PAGE 49

1. >; 2. <; 3. <; 4. <; 5. <; 6. <; 7. >; 8. <; 9. =; 10. >; 11. >; 12. >

PAGE 50

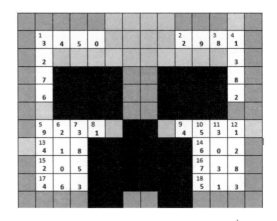

PAGE 51

1. 858; 2. 657; 3. 859; 4. 439; 5. 493; 6. 793; 7. 626; 8. 879; 9. 869

HIS FEET OFF THE FLOOR

PAGE 52

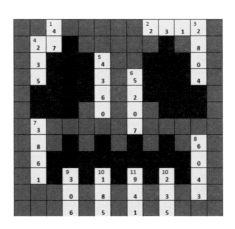

PAGE 53

1. 301; 2. 153; 3. 231; 4. 503;
5. 145; 6. 366; 7. 527; 8. 194; 9. 349

SEE OH DOUBLE YOU

PAGE 54

1.

	2	
4	1	6
	3	
	5	

2.

	1	
4	3	5
	2	
	6	

3.

	4	
6	5	2
	1	
	3	

PAGE 55

1. 600 animals; 2. 252 fish;
3. 195 baby polar bears; 4. 1,011 steps

PAGE 56

1. 12/35; 2. 9/8; 3. 13/36; 4. 7/10; 5. 9/18; 6. 15/56;
7. 14/45; 8. 11/28; 9. 7/12

PAGE 57

1. 40/56/48/24; 2. 20/35/45/10; 3. 18/6/8/14;
4. 3/0/7/9; 5. 4/24/32/8; 6. 49/28/35/63;
7. 48/30/6/36; 8. 9/72/0/27 9. 9/15/21/18

PAGE 58

1. 1/20, 10/2, 4/5, cross out 6 and 3; 2. 6/2, 12/1,
3/4, cross out 7 and 8; 3. 24/1, 6/4, 3/8, 2/12, no
numbers crossed out; 4. 9/4, 6/6, 2/18, 12/3, 1/36,
no numbers crossed out; 5. 7/6, 42/1, 3/14, 2/21,
cross out 8 and 9; 6. 1/25; 5/5, cross out 7, 2, and
both 9s; 7. 27/1, 9/3, cross out 7, 4, 2, and 6; 8.
5/7, 1/35, cross out 3, 15, 4, and 10; 9. 6/8, 3/16,
48/1, 12/4, 2/24, no numbers crossed out

PAGE 59

1. 1/12, 2/6, 3/4; 2. 1/15, 3/5; 3. 1/18, 2/9, 3/6;
4. 1/24, 2/12, 3/8, 4/6

PAGE 60

1.

3	6	13	4	7	9	43	31	6	8
1	9	15	2	21	5	75	22	10	98
17	53	19	18	35	24	29	40	2	11
46	83	16	26	13	23	27	28	71	62
89	44	95	47	52	65	38	30	70	57
20	78	55	88	14	67	86	33	51	49
59	74	14	42	93	73	77	36	39	68
12	52	22	61	50	25	80	54	37	42

2.

4	8	7	16	14	13	6	19	9	21
30	5	12	2	20	19	27	22	1	42
64	3	10	76	24	35	33	51	17	32
58	14	29	70	28	34	78	53	49	45
90	37	47	32	6	73	86	94	99	50
83	74	43	69	36	11	57	2	25	63
81	39	12	77	51	40	44	48	68	17
61	34	95	76	22	55	66	82	52	56

PAGE 61

1.

5	12	17	21	2	6	19	27	11	8
10	15	24	22	3	9	18	1	7	16
14	13	20	27	30	35	28	33	29	31
72	61	59	25	53	46	40	47	39	37
88	84	66	78	91	94	45	56	58	62
97	92	83	79	69	89	74	50	99	78
28	36	49	52	80	19	83	55	73	81
77	54	48	37	61	93	76	60	65	70

2.

9	18	32	11	31	7	49	8	18	21
1	2	27	3	6	67	19	20	47	36
14	39	40	36	45	10	4	9	5	12
38	29	25	17	54	44	76	13	55	53
50	89	82	15	60	63	98	73	69	70
62	12	28	97	85	79	72	81	37	64
49	21	46	95	23	77	86	66	90	83
84	13	67	30	52	88	80	57	42	99

PAGE 62

1. 45; 2. 450; 3. 450; 4. 4,500; 5. 24; 6. 240;
7. 240; 8. 2,400; 9. 42; 10. 420; 11. 420; 12. 4,200;
13. 4; 14. 40; 15. 40; 16. 400; 17. 18; 18. 180;
19. 180; 20. 1,800; 21. 35; 22. 350; 23. 350;
24. 3,500; 25. 48; 26. 480; 27. 480; 28. 4,800;
29. 12; 30. 120; 31. 120; 32. 1,200

PAGE 63

1. 240/2,400/24,000; 2. 150/1,500/15,000;
3. 270/2,700/27,000; 4. 360/3,600/36,000;
5. 420/4,200/42,000; 6. 610/6,100/61,000;
7. 580/5,800/58,000; 8. 730/7,300/73,000;
9. 860/8,600/86,000; 10. 900/9,000/90,000

PAGE 64

					23 x45			
			56 x16	33 x21	29 x19			
			49 x17	59 x16	15 x47			
	65 x61		64 x29	22 x44	37 x38			
		82 x40	11 x36	85 x62	18 x42		72 x54	
			98 x45	77 x69	61 x88	58 x58		
				59 x68				
				64 x93		44 x52		
		35 x58		53 x79	49 x47			
			59 x42	99 x99				
				83 x78				
		95 x38		64 x87		86 x45		
78 x51	86 x95		24 x89	73 x92	33 x65			43 x77
	73 x54	70 x85	90 x44	35 x60	66 x89	36 x85	53 x48	

PAGE 65

1. 621; 2. 2,080; 3. 1,978; 4. 750; 5. 4,828; 6. 2,142;
7. 713; 8. 676; 9. 1,749; 10. 1,428; 11. 810; 12. 1,452

HE HAD NO BODY TO GO WITH.

PAGE 66

PAGE 67

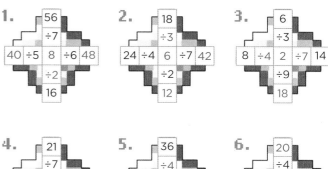

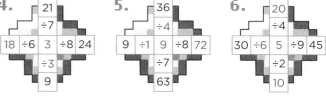

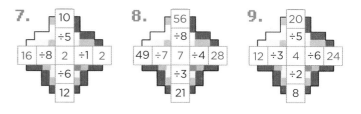

PAGE 68

1. 9 R2; 2. 7 R1; 3. 6 R6; 4. 9 R1; 5. 2 R4; 6. 4 R3;
7. 9 R3; 8. 5 R1; 9. 8 R1; 10. 5 R2; 11. 5 R6; 12. 4 R2;
13. 4 R1; 14. 3 R8; 15. 6 R2

SO IT COULD HAVE A PIGNIC.

PAGE 69

1. C; 2. A; 3. D; 4. B; 5. E

PAGE 70

1. 108 zombies; 2. 5 used 8 of the spawners and 6 used 1 of the spawners; 3. 76 creepers; 4. 90 husks

PAGE 71

1. 126 flowers; 2. 13 books were on 5 shelves and 12 were on 1 shelf; 3. 9 mooshrooms were spawned each day; 4. 2,320 apples

PAGE 72

Exact shading may vary, but number of spaces shaded in should match the examples below.

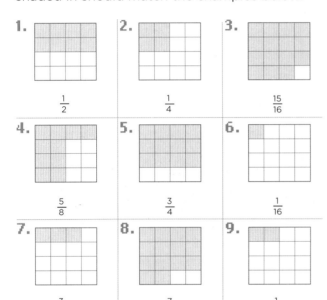

1. $\frac{1}{2}$ 2. $\frac{1}{4}$ 3. $\frac{15}{16}$

4. $\frac{5}{8}$ 5. $\frac{3}{4}$ 6. $\frac{1}{16}$

7. $\frac{3}{16}$ 8. $\frac{7}{8}$ 9. $\frac{1}{8}$

Order: $\frac{1}{16}$, $\frac{1}{8}$, $\frac{3}{16}$, $\frac{1}{4}$, $\frac{1}{2}$, $\frac{5}{8}$, $\frac{3}{4}$, $\frac{7}{8}$, $\frac{15}{16}$

PAGE 73

1. D; 2. A; 3. E; 4. B; 5. C

PAGE 74

1. $\frac{7}{9}$ 2. $\frac{8}{8}$ or 1 3. $\frac{5}{9}$ 4. $\frac{8}{9}$ 5. $\frac{3}{4}$ 6. $\frac{5}{6}$

PAGE 75

1. $\frac{3}{9}$ 2. $\frac{1}{8}$ 3. $\frac{2}{6}$ 4. $\frac{5}{9}$ 5. $\frac{3}{6}$ 6. $\frac{2}{8}$

PAGE 76

1. $1\frac{1}{2}$ 2. $\frac{2}{3}$ 3. $1\frac{1}{3}$ 4. $\frac{4}{6}$ 5. $1\frac{1}{4}$ 6. $\frac{2}{3}$

PAGE 77

1. $1\frac{1}{2}$ cups; 2. $\frac{4}{5}$ cup; 3 . 1 glistening melon;

4. $\frac{3}{4}$ cup of sugar

PAGE 78

1. .4; 2. .32; 3. .50; 4. .7; 5. .08; 6. .16; 7. .03; 8. .2; 9. .28; 10. .09
.03 / .7

PAGE 79

1. $\frac{6}{10}$, .6; 2. $\frac{28}{100}$, .28; 3. $\frac{3}{10}$, .3; 4. $\frac{6}{100}$, .06;

5. $\frac{56}{100}$, .56; 6. $\frac{81}{100}$, .81; 7. $\frac{1}{100}$, .01;

8. $\frac{1}{10}$, .1; 9. $\frac{58}{100}$, .58

PAGE 80

1. 1; 2. 3; 3. 6; 4. 10; 5. 15; 6. 21; 7. 28; 8. 36

PAGE 81

1. 9/9; 2. 25/34; 3. 49/83; 4. 81/164; 5. 11x11=121/285

PAGE 82

1. 36'; 2. 26'; 3. 40'; 4. 44'; 5. 32'; 6. 36'; 7. 12'; 8. 36'

PAGE 83

1. 9/4/36; 2. 5/4/20; 3. 6/5/30; 4. 8/1/8 5. 8/4/32; 6. 7/7/49

7. Length times width equals the area. l x w = a

PAGE 84

1. acute; 2. obtuse; 3. right; 4. right; 5. obtuse; 6. acute; 7. right; 8. obtuse; 9. right

PAGE 85

1. right; 2. acute; 3. acute; 4. right; 5. acute;
6. acute; 7. right; 8. right; 9. acute; 10. obtuse;
11. acute; 12. obtuse; 13. right; 14. right

PAGE 86

1. Parallel; 2. line; 3. line segment; 4. ray;
5. Intersecting; 6. point; 7. Perpendicular

PAGE 87

1. Answers will vary.   2.

3. 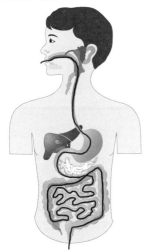   4. Dot to dot will show snow golem

PAGE 88

Answers will vary.

PAGE 89

1. nose; 2. mouth; 3. larynx; 4. trachea; 5. bronchi;
6. lungs; 7. diaphragm

PAGE 90

PAGE 91

Heart is the organ between lungs.
Veins are blue and lead to heart.
Arteries are red and lead away from heart.

PAGE 92

1. brain; 2. spinal cord; 3. nerves

PAGE 93

PAGE 95

PAGE 96

Answers will vary.

PAGE 97

1. ocelot: predator; cod: prey; 2. shark: predator;
fish: prey; 3. frog: predator; fly: prey; 4. snake:
predator; eggs: prey; 5. wolf: predator; rabbit:
prey; 6. bird: predator; worm: prey

PAGE 98

1. D; 2. F; 3. A; 4. E; 5. B; 6. C

PAGE 99

1. leopard; 2. zebra; 3. praying mantis; 4. owl;
5. toad; 6. seahorse

PAGE 100

Things that will sink: potato, bone, cobblestone
block, egg. Things that will float: feather, bee,
apple, cobweb.

PAGE 101

1. molecules; 2. gas; 3. liquid; 4. solid

PAGE 102

Every potion needs: glass bottle, water, Nether wart, and Awkward potion.

PAGE 103

1. Potion of Swiftness, potion of Leaping, potion of Strength, potion of Healing; 2. sugar; 3. rabbit's foot; 4. blaze powder; 5. glistering melon; 6. Answers will vary.

PAGE 104

1. crust; 2. mantle; 3. outer core; 4. inner core

PAGE 105

PAGE 106

	granite	clay	quartz	sandstone
soft		✔		✔
hard	✔		✔	✔
permeable (liquid **can** pass through)				✔
nonpermeable (liquid **cannot** pass through)	✔	✔	✔	
shiny	✔		✔	
dull		✔		✔

PAGE 107

1. C; 2. A; 3. D; 4. B

PAGE 108

PAGE 109

1. fault; 2. epicenter; 3. seismic waves; 4. focus

PAGE 110

Answers will vary.

PAGE 111

1. F; 2. T; 3. F; 4. F; 5. T; 6. F

PAGE 112

1. First an earthquake occurs below the ocean.
2. A section of the ocean floor rises or falls.
3. The ocean water rises or falls. 4. Large waves form. 5. Large waves hit the shore.

PAGE 113

PAGE 114

The magnet will attract the iron nail, steel paper clip, and iron ore.

PAGE 115

1. repel; 2. repel; 3. attract; 4. repel; 5. attract; 6. repel

PAGES 116 AND 117

Answers will vary.

PAGE 118

1. device; 2. source; 3. conductor; 4. switch

PAGE 119

1. There is not a complete circuit. 2. The switch is in the off position.

PAGE 120

1. E; 2. B; 3. A; 4. D; 5. C

PAGES 121-124

Answers will vary.

PAGE 125

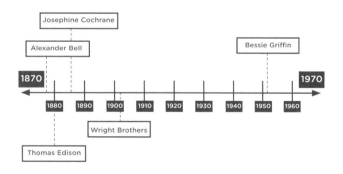

PAGE 126

```
S V A S C O N U N E Z D E B A L B O A
Q U B O S E T R O C N A N R E H F Z J
E K B R R K J T L Z K N T M E J N N
Q K X M B R R B P L P Q N V R T Y Z L
V Q A Q U K A P T X Y T T D Z J G B J
Y A B R M L G Z M R T J V U Y B N B
X Y S Z D J O Y I D L N R A Z R L Y M
R K M C R S W C B P A M N M D X J V Z
Y L D X O N I W R N O P L Z J L Y Q D
N D L L T D R C D E O C Z N M B T J K
D Y L Q D B A M N N H T S Z Z N G O G
D Y L L B R A G C A Y P W I J J X V V
K W L J N G J E A J R M O B C O M N D
R M D Y E Q D B T M Y F P T P N D Y J
Z T L L V E X W T B A Z R O S L A Y P
R G L B L M Y X T B K W C I D I K R L
J A Y E J Y Y B P Q M R T X S X R G F
N R O M M Y Q M Y R A L N R X K V H N
V N B Q L Q N D R M T Y L T X N B P C
```

PAGE 127

1. 34 or 35 men were on each ship; 2. almost 5 months; 3. about 41 miles per day; 4. 13,896 more Powhatan Indians

PAGE 128

1. B; 2. E; 3. A; 4. D; 5. C

PAGE 129

1. New Hampshire; 2. New York; 3. Massachusetts; 4. Rhode Island; 5. Connecticut; 6. New Jersey; 7. Pennsylvania; 8. Delaware; 9. Maryland; 10. Virginia; 11. North Carolina; 12. South Carolina; 13. Georgia

PAGE 130

1. D; 2. B; 3. A; 4. C

PAGE 131

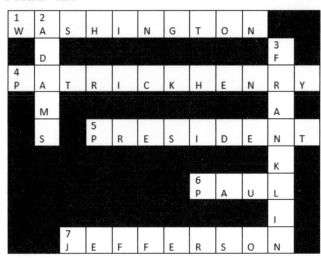

PAGE 132

Answers will vary.

PAGE 133

```
      C H O C T A W
      C R E E K
C H I C K A S A W
      C H E R O K E E
      S E M I N O L E
```

PAGE 134-137

Answers will vary.

PAGE 138

1. Canada; 2. Pacific Ocean and Arctic Ocean;
3. Bering Sea, Chukchi Sea, and Beaufort Sea;
4. Answers will vary.

PAGE 139

1. Niihau; 2. Kauai; 3. Oahu; 4. Molokai; 5. Lanai;
6. Maui; 7. Hawaii

PAGE 140-142

Answers will vary.

PAGE 143

1. Ocean; 2. Arctic; 3. Swamp; 4. Village; 5. Desert;
6. Farm

PAGE 144

1. 150°; 2. 100°; 3. 50°; 4. 100°; 5. 150°; 6. 70°;
7. 30°; 8. 40°; 9. 60°

PAGE 145

1. longitude lines; 2. latitude lines; 3. equator;
4. prime meridian; 5. United States; 6. Australia;
7. Africa; 8. Asia

PAGE 146

Answers may include:
globe: round; 3-D model; shows the whole
planet; shaped like a sphere; map: flat; used for
directions; has a title; both: shows oceans; has a
key; shows relationship of places

PAGE 147 AND 148

Answers will vary.

PAGE 149

1. good; 2. service; 3. service; 4. service; 5. good;
6. good; 7. good; 8. service